DEAR READER,

It's common to learn a concept or two from some of the books you read that you can apply to your life, but those concepts rarely move the needle. My goal with this book is much bigger than that—it's to **change your life**. I know, that's a big goal, but house hacking *is* that powerful. I've experienced it myself and I'm confident that you can, and will, do the same.

Life-changing doesn't mean that it'll make you a millionaire overnight. It takes hard work and sacrifice. Whether it's financial freedom, riches, or something in between, if you're willing to put in the work necessary to learn and **implement the strategy** of house hacking, you can set yourself up for the life you've always wanted. The keyword there is "implement." Just learning the material in this book won't do anything for you. You have to actually take what you learned and apply it to your life. I've learned it myself—don't get stuck in the Infinite Learning Loop. Take action.

And finally, I know personal finance is typically a taboo subject that is avoided in most conversations. I've often found myself **wanting to help** and teach others about house hacking, but felt it wasn't really appropriate for me to do so. Now, I simply gift them this book and allow them to do as they wish with it. If you find yourself in a similar situation, consider doing the same. It might just change someone's life.

Get to work,
Robert Leonard
@therobertleonard

WELCOME TO THE EVERYTHING® SERIES!

These handy, accessible books give you all you need to tackle a difficult project, gain a new hobby, comprehend a fascinating topic, prepare for an exam, or even brush up on something you learned back in school but have since forgotten.

You can choose to read an Everything® book from cover to cover or just pick out the information you want from our four useful boxes: Questions, Facts, Alerts, and Essentials. We give you everything you need to know on the subject, but throw in a lot of fun stuff along the way too.

QUESTION
Answers to common questions.

FACT
Important snippets of information.

ALERT
Urgent warnings.

ESSENTIAL
Quick handy tips.

We now have more than 600 Everything® books in print, spanning such wide-ranging categories as cooking, health, parenting, personal finance, wedding planning, word puzzles, and so much more. When you're done reading them all, you can finally say you know Everything®!

PUBLISHER Karen Cooper

MANAGING EDITOR Lisa Laing

COPY CHIEF Casey Ebert

PRODUCTION EDITOR Jo-Anne Duhamel

ACQUISITIONS EDITOR Rachel Thatcher

DEVELOPMENT EDITOR Brett Palana-Shanahan

EVERYTHING® SERIES COVER DESIGNER Erin Alexander

Live for free, earn passive income, and build wealth with your own home

THE **EVERYTHING**®
GUIDE TO
HOUSE HACKING

YOUR STEP-BY-STEP GUIDE TO:
- Financing a House Hack
- Finding Ideal Properties and Tenants
- Maximizing the Profitability of Your Property
- Navigating the Real Estate Market
- Avoiding Unnecessary Risk

ROBERT LEONARD

Adams Media

New York   London   Toronto   Sydney   New Delhi

To Brayden, you give me motivation and reason to chase my dreams.
To Dad, you taught me it was possible, and made it so.
To Meme, your love, support, and unwavering faith are invaluable.
Any good I do or am is because of you three. Thank you.

Adams Media
An Imprint of Simon & Schuster, Inc.
100 Technology Center Drive
Stoughton, Massachusetts 02072

An Everything® Series Book.

Everything® and everything.com® are registered trademarks of Simon & Schuster, Inc.

First Adams Media trade paperback edition September 2022

ADAMS MEDIA and colophon are trademarks of Simon & Schuster.

For information about special discounts for bulk purchases, please contact Simon & Schuster Special Sales at 1-866-506-1949 or business@simonandschuster.com.

The Simon & Schuster Speakers Bureau can bring authors to your live event. For more information or to book an event contact the Simon & Schuster Speakers Bureau at 1-866-248-3049 or visit our website at www.simonspeakers.com.

Manufactured in the United States of America

1 2022

Library of Congress Cataloging-in-Publication Data
Names: Leonard, Robert, author.
Title: The everything® guide to house hacking / Robert Leonard.
Description: Stoughton, Massachusetts: Adams Media, 2022 | Series: Everything® series | Includes index.
Identifiers: LCCN 2022014637 | ISBN 9781507217191 (pb) | ISBN 9781507217207 (ebook)
Subjects: LCSH: Real estate investment. | Home ownership. | Rental housing.
Classification: LCC HD1382.5 .L455 2022 | DDC 332.63/24--dc23/eng/20220328
LC record available at https://lccn.loc.gov/2022014637

ISBN 978-1-5072-1719-1
ISBN 978-1-5072-1720-7 (ebook)

CONTENTS

INTRODUCTION

- Are you looking to grow your wealth?
- Do you want to reduce your housing costs and even live for free?
- Are you hoping to build your financial future with little money down?

Then house hacking may be what you've been looking for! House hacking is a real estate investing strategy where you use a residential property to earn income. It is a simple plan for building your wealth that takes very little money up front and allows you to reap the rewards of financial freedom. And the best part is, *anyone* can do it!

House hacking is often accomplished by purchasing a property, living in a portion of it, and renting out the remaining area with the goal of reducing your living expenses or potentially even profiting. But house hacking is not limited to that one model; you can also accomplish it through situations such as live-in flips, finding roommates for your current home, owning multiple properties, vacation rentals, and even participating in the sharing economy with Airbnb.

Not only will house hacking significantly improve your financial position by reducing what is probably your largest expense (your home); it is also a way to get started in real estate investing without a lot of money. That being said, house hacking is not fancy or flashy, and it won't make you wealthy overnight. However, house hacking *can*: Increase your investing returns, shorten your time to financial freedom, teach you to become a landlord with training wheels on, provide you with multiple tax benefits, and much, much more!

With *The Everything® Guide to House Hacking*, you'll learn:

- Why house hacking is a smart wealth-building strategy
- How house hacking can work with almost anyone's situation
- How to analyze, find, acquire, and/or manage a house hack
- Who is needed on your real estate team and how to build it
- The right steps to buying and financing your property
- How to find and professionally manage tenants

Most importantly, house hacking will open you up to an entirely new world of possibilities! Even if you've never purchased or invested in real estate, this book can help you understand and manage properties in a way that will forever change your financial position. House hacking lets you build the future you've always dreamed of!

CHAPTER 1

House Hacking 101

If you build a house on a weak foundation, it is unlikely to stand the test of time. Whether that foundation is weak because not enough time was spent on understanding how to build it correctly, construction was rushed, or the wrong materials were used, the outcome is the same. The same can be said about investing. If you don't take the time to understand the strategies thoroughly, rush the process, or learn from the wrong sources of information, you are likely to have bad results. In this chapter, you'll build a strong foundation by learning about what house hacking is, who it is and isn't good for, what you need to know about your personal finances to get started, and how to set goals and expectations for house hacking.

What Is House Hacking?

House hacking is a strategy whereby you use a residential property as an investment. When house hacking, you are making the property an asset for yourself, rather than a liability, which is the traditional situation for most homeowners. The most common way to house hack is to purchase a property with four units or fewer, live in a portion of it, and rent out the remaining area, with the goal of reducing your personal living expenses or potentially even profiting. House hacking can also involve finding roommates for your current home or renting all or part of your home on a short-term basis with a service like Airbnb. The main goal of house hacking is to cover some or all of your mortgage through other renters and not completely from your own pocket.

Is a Home Your "Greatest" Asset?

It is often assumed that your home is your greatest asset. But is that a fact or just a common misconception? Putting aside the debate of "greatest," is one's home even an asset? One of the most well-known real estate investors and bestselling real estate authors, Robert Kiyosaki, argues that one's home is not an asset; rather it is actually a liability. Kiyosaki keeps the definition of and difference between assets and liabilities simple. Assets are anything that generates cash for you, while liabilities are anything that takes cash from you.

ESSENTIAL

Realize that, in the traditional sense, a house is a liability. Just because many people believe the common narrative that a house is an asset, this does not make it true. Reframing the way you view assets and liabilities can have a substantial impact on your financial future.

As you will see throughout this book, the unconventional wealth-building strategies, hard work, and sacrifice that are required for house hacking are not for everyone—and that is okay. However, for those of you who are ready to learn the wealth-building strategy of house hacking, it is crucial to understand that assets put money back in your pocket and liabilities take money from your pocket.

Traditional Home Buying

Most homeowners follow the traditional strategy of purchasing a house at or above their maximum budget, leading to a large monthly mortgage payment for the next fifteen, twenty, or thirty years. This process typically begins by having a conversation with a lender or mortgage broker to discover how much you can afford. You are asked for your and your spouse's monthly income as well as your debt payments, which allows the banker to calculate your debt-to-income ratio.

FACT

Debt-to-income (DTI) ratio is a percentage calculated by dividing your total monthly debt payments by your total gross monthly income. This can be calculated on an individual basis or combined with co-borrowers if applying jointly.

Most institutions have their own guidelines for an acceptable DTI level. If you have ever discussed loan application processes with anyone, you probably know at least one person who was denied for a loan, whether it was a mortgage or a different product, due to a DTI that was too high and above the lender's threshold.

Once the banker has your DTI, they will "back into" the amount for which you are eligible to be approved for your preapproval letter. Essentially, they can now tell you the mortgage amount they believe you can afford.

ESSENTIAL

The maximum amount you are approved for during a lender's preapproval process and/or the underwriting process may not be what you can actually afford. It may be what you can "afford" on paper, in the eyes of the lender, but in the real world, you probably will not be able to afford the mortgage payment prescribed for you.

At this point, most people are ecstatic—they have just been preapproved to buy a home, and they can finally start shopping. Unfortunately, this is where the problems usually begin to pile up.

Too often, someone following a traditional strategy will set out to spend less than they were approved for because that is the "right" thing to do. Then reality sets in. They start searching for homes to purchase, and, of course, those that are toward the top of their budget are nicer, in better locations, and have just the right lighting to grow their special plants or the perfect area for their dog to rest. Not only are they now looking at homes toward the top of their budget; so is everyone else, and a bidding war breaks out. To get that perfect dream home, you have to go back to your lender and get approved for just a bit more money so that you can submit an above-asking offer.

Market conditions and real estate markets across the globe will dictate the competitive nature of any real estate transaction, but the situation just described is very common in many US real estate markets, barring a recession. The people in our scenario now own a home that is not only pushing their limits; it is also purely a liability—it only takes from their pocket. Their monthly payment of mortgage principal, interest, taxes, insurance, and, potentially, private mortgage insurance is taking money from their pocket, and there is no source of income from that property to put money back into their pocket. Many people wrongly believe their home is their largest asset, but you should reconsider that notion—is a traditional home truly an asset?

FACT

Private mortgage insurance (PMI) is an insurance premium that borrowers are often required to pay if they purchase a property using a loan with less than 20 percent as a down payment. PMI protects the lender, not the buyer, in the event payments stop, as the lender sees a smaller down payment as a higher-risk loan.

Putting aside the appeal of cash entering your pocket versus cash leaving your pocket, which is hard to argue against, many traditional homeowners will maintain that their home is an asset because of appreciation. Over the mortgage period, the home is paid off and is one day owned free and clear, and it can then be sold for a large amount and often a gain in appreciation. This is the common argument made by traditional homeowners. Before you decide if that makes sense to you, let's take a deeper look.

Opportunity Cost

Opportunity cost is one of the most important considerations in one's life, yet it is arguably one of the most ignored concepts. When you choose one option over another, the option you did not choose is your *opportunity cost*. It can often be monetary, but it does not have to be. Here are two concrete examples to make this even more clear—one where the monetary situation makes no impact on the decision, and one where the situation is almost purely monetary.

Say you have to choose between going to a concert on a Friday night with your friends or taking your significant other to dinner. Assuming the concert tickets cost about the same as your meal and travel, you are financially indifferent about which you choose. However, from a nonmonetary perspective, you may prefer one situation over the other for an infinite number of reasons, all of which have nothing to do with money. If you choose the concert with your friends, your opportunity cost is that you miss out on a dinner date with your significant other. If you pass on the concert and have your dinner date, now the concert is your opportunity cost. This opportunity cost exists because you cannot be in two places at the same time.

Similarly, you cannot spend or invest the same dollar in more than one place at the same time. Let's assume you have $10,000 that you have saved and are ready to use. Your plan is to either use the $10,000 as your down payment on a home or invest in the stock market. You find the perfect home and can acquire it for a purchase price of $200,000, using your $10,000 as a 5 percent down payment. (For the sake of simplicity, we will assume that you have no closing costs and are setting no money aside for reserves. You can be all-in for $10,000 even.) The home was truly your dream home, and you lived there for thirty years. It is now thirty years in the future, and you have a beautiful, paid-off home.

The real estate market where you purchased your home has done well, having appreciated roughly 2–3 percent per year on average since you acquired the property. Your property is now worth between $362,000 and $485,000. Not bad for a $10,000 investment, huh?

Not so fast. What about the mortgage payments you had been making for thirty years? That money needs to be considered in your return equation, yet it is often overlooked. Over the thirty years, you would have paid $190,000 toward principal to pay down the loan, $98,387.71 for interest and roughly $72,000 for taxes and insurance. Did the home actually only cost $10,000? Not quite—you had to pay $370,387 in cash out of your pocket just to fully own the property. If your property is worth the lower end of the range mentioned previously, you would have lost approximately $8,000 over thirty years. If your property is worth the higher end of the aforementioned range, you would have made approximately $115,000 over thirty years.

What about repairs and maintenance? Anyone who is currently or previously has been a homeowner knows that the list of things to fix in a home is never ending—and costly. A relatively safe and conservative assumption for repairs and maintenance over thirty years is $50,000. Your loss of $8,000 just became a loss of $58,000, and your potential gain of $115,000 has shrunk to $65,000. Most people would see a paid-off house worth between $362,000 and $485,000, mistakenly think they had only paid $200,000 for it, and therefore believe they had made a handsome profit. In reality, however, the situation is quite different.

This is all without any consideration of the all-important opportunity cost previously discussed. When you take opportunity cost into consideration, the financial picture becomes even worse. Remember that you had two options with your $10,000? You could use it as a down payment on a house or invest it in the stock market. Let's look at how the latter situation would have played out.

Instead of putting the $10,000 into a traditional home as a down payment, you choose to rent. You find a nice apartment for $750 per month, which allows you to invest the $10,000 in the stock market, and you can also save $250 per month, since your rent is lower than your mortgage payment by this amount. You also invest this in the stock market. Over the thirty-year period in which you would have owned the home, you instead invested a total of $100,000, earned $505,000 in gains from an average annual return of 9 percent, and had a total investment balance of $605,000.

The difference between your true profit at the end of thirty years of homeownership and the gains earned on your stock market investments is your opportunity cost. This is the amount of money you would have forgone by purchasing a home instead of renting and investing in the stock market.

> **ALERT**
>
> Both the ending value of your home and the value of your stock portfolio—and therefore the corresponding opportunity cost values—are highly sensitive to the rate of growth used in the computations. A swing in either direction, up or down, can significantly impact the results.

House Hacking Is a Better Way

House hacking is a solution to the problem of opportunity cost. The previous examples and the discussion of opportunity cost should get your wheels turning and cause you to begin challenging the societal norms you have learned related to money. Now consider this: In the traditional strategy of purchasing a home to live in, is your home truly an asset? How has your opinion on the matter of asset versus liability changed after reading the previous few paragraphs?

House hacking can take shape by using different property types, such as single-family homes, duplexes, triplexes, and fourplexes, as well as different sub-strategies, such as live-in flips, vacation properties, and even RVs! Not only do various property types and sub-strategies exist; you can also mix and match them to create numerous ways to implement a house hacking strategy. Your creativity is the only limitation on the possibilities of house hacking.

Each of these property types and sub-strategies will be discussed in detail in later chapters, but for now, it is important to understand the general idea of what house hacking is and that there is likely a strategy that works for nearly anyone reading this book.

FACT

People have been house hacking in many different ways over the past few decades, but Brandon Turner of *BiggerPockets* officially named the strategy "house hacking" years ago.

Who Is House Hacking Good For?

After hearing about the previous examples of opportunity costs, it may be difficult to rationalize or understand why someone would not house hack. If you are reading this book, you probably already agree that there is a better way than the traditional strategies used by most people. Maybe you see most people living a life you do not want to live, which has led you to search for a better way, or maybe there is something intuitive inside you that tells you there must be another path.

Arguably the most common reason, or limiting belief, potential real estate investors give for why they do not get started in real estate is insufficient funds or a lack of capital. Others state it is because they lack the experience and, therefore, confidence to buy real estate. If this is you, house hacking is a great fit. You can purchase a property with a 3.5–5 percent down payment, and potentially with even no money down by using VA (Veterans Affairs) loans and other specialized 0 percent down loan products. Most traditional investment properties require a minimum of 10 percent down or, more often than not, closer to 20–25 percent as your down payment. House hacking has been called a way to learn real estate investing with training wheels or by starting with the "lite" version. Instead of investing in a large multifamily property such as an apartment building with dozens of tenants, you can start with just a few tenants. The ability to make a much smaller down payment on a property and learning the process with just a few tenants makes house hacking a great option for those without a lot of money or experience, and makes it a much simpler way to get started as a real estate investor.

House hacking is probably a great fit for the person who is looking to supercharge their wealth-building process, is willing to sacrifice in the short term for long-term gains, and is looking to build passive income. For the everyday person, house hacking is one of the best ways not only to improve your odds of becoming wealthy but also to make the process as efficient (quick and easy) as possible.

ALERT

Very few things in this life are guaranteed. While the probability of generating wealth from house hacking is significantly higher than going the traditional path of homeownership, it is not guaranteed. House hacking is also not a get-rich-quick scheme, nor will it lead to massive success overnight. Great things take time, and house hacking is no different.

Just because house hacking makes the process more efficient, quicker, and easier, that does not mean you will not have to make sacrifices—you absolutely will. House hacking is right for the person who can temporarily put aside their wants in the short term to achieve what they want in the long term. As a house hacker, you will probably have to sacrifice the quality of the property you live in or the neighborhood where you buy. It is uncommon for a house hacker to have the best of both worlds—their dream home while house hacking.

There is a relationship between the amount of comfort you give up and a property's profitability when it comes to house hacking. Imagine a graph with the amount of comfort you give up on the x-axis and profitability on the y-axis. As you move toward the right on the x-axis, you increase the amount of comfort you are sacrificing. However, as you move right on the x-axis, you also move up on the y-axis, meaning you are increasing your profitability. Every house hacker's situation is going to be different when determining how much comfort needs to be sacrificed to gain profitability. Real estate markets across the country will cause this to vary from location to location—some markets may require less sacrifice than other markets. The relationship between the amount of comfort given up and the property's profitability will remain the same across all markets, just in varying degrees.

ESSENTIAL

In areas where property values are higher, such as major cities and the East and West Coasts in the United States, more comfort must be given up in order to achieve more profitability. Areas where property values are lower and/or rent-to-purchase price is higher, less comfort has to be given up to gain more profitability. The strategy and property type also have an impact on the degree to which the relationship stands.

You will likely need to have uncomfortable conversations with your significant other, friends, and family members who may not understand what you are doing and why you are doing it. House hacking is good for people who are willing to give up a few years of comfort and short-term goals of owning a dream home and having tough conversations with their loved ones for the long-term pleasure of passive income and financial freedom.

Who Isn't House Hacking Good For?

House hacking is *possible* for nearly everyone, but the truth is, it is not a good fit for everyone. House hacking may not be good for someone who is a short-term thinker, extremely risk-averse, does not want to be a landlord or have investment exposure to real estate, or someone whose co-borrower (a roommate or significant other) is not on board.

As was discussed in the previous sections, sacrifices will have to be made to be a successful house hacker. Typically, these sacrifices are made for a minimum of one year to upward of five to seven years, although there is no cap. This will be hard for someone who focuses on the short term and thinks in weeks and months rather than years. As with nearly any investment or real estate transaction, there is inherent risk involved. Someone who can't sleep at night knowing they own investments—and the associated underlying risks—is probably not the right person to house hack. If your investments keep you up at night, it is probably not worth the financial gain you could receive.

Whether it is the inherent increased risk from being a landlord or some other aspect, if you are not comfortable with being a landlord, house hacking is probably not right for you. There are ways (discussed later) to remove yourself from the actual process of being a landlord, but there is always some involvement.

It can also be difficult to house hack successfully if you face too much pushback from important people in your life. This is often an issue between significant others, where one is willing to make the sacrifices necessary to house hack, while the other is not. However, this is not the only relationship issue that can arise with house hacking. Depending on your dynamic with parents or friends, their potential hesitation toward house hacking or their attempts to steer you in a different direction could make house hacking difficult for you. This is not to say that someone dealing with these relationship dynamics cannot house hack, but it may not be the perfect fit.

Understanding Your Personal Finances

Personal finance is the foundation for any investing strategy, house hacking included. As mentioned previously, if you attempt to build a house on a weak foundation or try to implement investment strategies without a strong personal finance base, both will have the same result—ruin. Houses built on a weak foundation may last for a short period, but they are unlikely to stand the test of time. The same goes for investing. You may be able to implement your investing strategies for a few months or maybe even a few years, but it is unlikely you will be able to sustain those strategies for the long term without first building your strong foundation—your personal finances.

Your Budget

The first place to begin when building this personal finance base is with your budget—both where you are currently and where you want your budget to go. Before you can know where you want to go, you have to know where you currently stand. There are numerous online platforms that can help you understand your current budget. You can create an account, link your bank information, and begin categorizing your transactions. Once your transactions have been categorized, you can review where your money is going each month. For those who are less tech-savvy, you can ask your local bank or credit union for a printout of your most recent statements, then complete the same activity—categorize all your transactions and review where your money is going each month.

Once you know where your money is going each month, you can compare that to where you want your money to actually go. If you keep spending in alignment with your current habits, will you reach your financial goals? Will you be able to save enough money to buy a house hack within your preferred time frame? If not, consider where changes are needed and begin making them immediately.

ALERT

Following a budget should not feel restrictive, nor should you feel it is taking away your ability to spend money on things that make you happy. It should be quite the contrary—your budget should be freeing and used as a tool to help you buy more of the things you actually want.

According to Ramit Sethi's book *I Will Teach You to Be Rich*, your budget should be broken down into three main buckets—savings and investing, fixed costs, and guilt-free spending money. Each of these buckets needs to be assigned a percentage, and the three buckets combined must equal 100 percent. You may start with 30 percent for savings and investing, 20 percent for guilt-free spending money, and 50 percent for fixed costs as your baseline, and adjust accordingly based on what you believe to be most realistic given your current financial situation. Each bucket can be subsequently broken down into smaller buckets if you prefer to get more detailed. For example, savings and investment may be made up of multiple goals, such as saving for a down payment on a house hack and buying a wedding ring, which combined equal 30 percent of your income. The same goes for fixed costs and guilt-free spending.

Remember discussing how much house you can truly afford? Following the rules just laid out for you, your mortgage payments would fall into the fixed costs bucket and would need to be less than 30 percent of your income. You will also need to use the savings and investing bucket of 30 percent to save for your down payment and reserves for your house hack, which will be discussed in more detail later. If any of these buckets' percentages are out of line and do not have you on a path toward achieving your goals, make the necessary changes as soon as possible.

To determine if your percentages are out of line, you need to first categorize all of your monthly expenses. This can be done manually by printing out your bank statement for the most recent month, or you can connect your bank accounts to an online budgeting tool. Whichever strategy you choose, the process is the same—categorize every transaction you had that month into one of your buckets, then divide the total amount for each bucket by your total monthly income. For example, if you had a total of $3,000 in fixed costs and your monthly income was $4,000, your fixed cost bucket would be 75 percent. In order to get that percentage down to your target of 50 percent, you would need to eliminate monthly expenses you currently have that equal 25 percent of your monthly income, which would be $1,000 in the previous example.

Typically housing costs, whether rent or a mortgage, are the largest portion of one's fixed cost bucket. If that is the case for you house hacking can help significantly reduce your fixed costs percentage. Some of the decisions you will need to make to reduce your expenses below your bucket's goal percentage, whichever bucket it is, are not easy. Your long-term will to achieve financial freedom must be stronger than your short-term pleasure of the unnecessary expenses.

Your Credit Score

Albeit a major component of your personal finances, your budget is just one piece of building your larger foundation. Another important component of your foundation and, ultimately, your house hacking journey, is your credit score. Few people know what their credit score is, and even fewer know what it actually consists of.

> **FACT**
>
> There are three official credit bureaus that formulate their own credit score—TransUnion, Equifax, and Experian. Each credit bureau uses similar information from your credit reports as part of their calculations, but each uses slightly different formulas. Lenders can use credit scores from whichever bureau they prefer, or they can even request your score from more than one.

A credit score is a three-digit number used by lenders to assess your credit risk. In the case of a house hack, a lender uses your credit score to determine how likely you are to make your mortgage payments on time and then bases your interest rate on that. Your credit score is calculated using a formula that derives its input values from the information in your credit report—a comprehensive overview of all credit-related products you have had in the past. The six input values typically included in credit score formulas are the percentage of payments you have made on time, how much of your available credit you are using, how many derogatory accounts you have had, the average length of your credit history, the total number of credit accounts you have had, and how many hard inquiries you have had.

As with a budget, the first step in getting your credit score to where it needs to be to achieve your financial goals is to understand where you are right now. Thankfully, many sites will give you free, comprehensive access to your credit score and your credit report. Begin with a trusted resource, such as Credit Karma, that can give you your credit score and the details of your report. Most sites that provide this information will also provide guidance on why you are where you are currently and what scores are considered good, bad, or somewhere in the middle. Review this information and see your current position. In addition to seeing where you are for the six major items, you can also review the information listed in your credit report. It is important to check for any inaccurate information or missing items.

> **ESSENTIAL**
>
> The exact percentage that each item impacts your score varies among credit bureaus, but typically your payment history, credit limit use, and derogatory accounts are considered high impact, the average age of your credit accounts is considered medium impact, and your total number of accounts and hard inquiries are considered low impact.

With a budget, you can make changes immediately. You can decide you are no longer going to spend money on certain items and start shifting your money into other buckets. You can start working on credit scores right away, but it takes longer for situations to actually change. Because of this, it is very important to begin working on building or fixing your credit score well in advance of when you need to. It will be difficult to purchase a house hack next month if you have no or bad credit history. However, if you begin now, you should be able to make the necessary changes to your credit score over the next three to six months, which will put you in a position to be approved for a mortgage.

Setting Goals and Expectations

As humans, our reaction to a certain situation is often far more important than the situation or problem itself. It is not what happens to you that matters but how you react to it that makes all the difference. Expectations play a key role in this equation. Even if the outcome of a situation is positive, if it is not as positive as you expected, you will probably feel the outcome was actually negative. If you were expecting to get $100 in a birthday card as a gift, but you received $20 instead, you will probably not be happy or satisfied with the $20 outcome because you were expecting $100—despite now having $20 more than you did before.

When it comes to house hacking, if you do not have the right expectations going in, regardless of how good the outcome is, you may not be satisfied. To avoid disappointment, it is important to set realistic expectations before you make any decisions. The first step in setting your expectations is to define your goal for your house hack. Are you looking to simply reduce your largest expense, your housing costs, or do you want to actually make a profit each month? Are you trying to get a rental property by using an owner-occupied loan for a year? Do you realize this property may not match exactly with what you envision as your forever home? How long do you plan on living in the property?

Once you have defined your goals for your house hack, you can begin looking for a property that will help you achieve those goals, while also setting expectations for the acquisition phase. Set expectations for how much money you will need to close on a deal and a property type by determining what the real estate market is like in your area. Is the market competitive with everything going over asking price, or are properties sitting in the multiple listing service (MLS) database for longer than average? Use these questions to set your expectations for what your experience may be like when making offers on potential properties.

Not only must you set expectations with yourself; you must also do so with other parties involved. This will include your co-borrower (if you have one), possibly your friends and family, and possibly even your real estate agent. If you are going to be living in the property with another person, it is important that each of you discuss your wants and needs and set expectations with each other. Your friends and family may not be the deciding factor in what you buy or how you buy it, but you can avoid potentially awkward and difficult conversations by discussing your plans for house hacking with your friends and family up front. If you explain to them what you are doing and why, their expectations will be in line with your plans for the near future. Then when things actually start to come together, they will not be surprised when you purchase a duplex or triplex in a mediocre part of town. Your real estate agent likely works more with traditional homeowners than they do with investors, and specifically house hackers, so it is a good idea to chat with them about your goals and expectations when searching for a property to purchase. Your agent can assist you; they just need to set their expectations appropriately for a house hacker, not a traditional homeowner.

For the last phase of setting expectations, it is important to spend some time thinking about what it is going to be like living in your new home. It has been mentioned throughout this chapter, but it's worth repeating: House hacking requires sacrifice. Setting your expectations up front about your living conditions while house hacking allows you to have a more pleasurable experience in a potentially less-than-optimal situation when it comes to comfort. It is also important to have an exit strategy. In Chapter 13, you'll learn about your options for exiting a house hack and spend time reflecting on what you plan to do when you are done house hacking. Are you going to move out, rent the property as a traditional rental, and house hack again? What if house hacking isn't for you; what are the next steps? How long must you legally stay in the property? By setting realistic expectations up front for all phases of house hacking, you are taking the first steps in ensuring a rewarding experience on your way to financial freedom.

CHAPTER 2

The Benefits of House Hacking

When considering ways to build wealth, there are few strategies as powerful as house hacking. It is flexible and can be made to work in nearly any situation for nearly any person. It's a proven strategy with a repeatable blueprint. It is not a get-rich-quick scheme, but it is one of the highest-probability, highest-impact strategies everyday people can implement to build wealth. House hacking is a true supercharger for your wealth-building machine. In this chapter, you'll learn how you can start house hacking with your current home, use house hacking to reduce your largest expense, get started without a lot of money, and even shorten your time until retirement.

Starting with Your Current Home

You may be wondering if house hacking is possible for you if you already own your home. The short answer is yes, it is. It may not be the perfect house hacking situation, nor may it fit your house hacking goals exactly, but it *is* possible. You have not missed the proverbial house hacking boat just because you already own a home. You will learn the exact strategies available to you when house hacking with your current home later in this chapter, but for now, it is important to realize that you are not ineligible for house hacking just because you own a home that you did not initially design to house hack.

ESSENTIAL

House hacking is a strategy whereby you rent out space in your home that is not currently being used or could be used more efficiently. Whether you bought your current home as an investment designed to house hack or not, you do not have to purchase an entirely new property to begin house hacking.

Being able to house hack with your current home is a benefit for a few reasons. It allows you to test the waters of house hacking before jumping in with both feet, it saves you from having to move from a home and/or area you like, and it allows you to avoid the selling and purchasing process or having to save up money for a down payment and closing costs.

Whether you are buying a home using the traditional approach or are house hacking, making a real estate purchase is a big decision. Purchasing real estate is rarely a permanent situation, and there are many exit strategies, but even still, the process can be costly and time consuming if you make a mistake. By using your current home, you can test house hacking before you go all-in. Presumably, you have been living in your home for some time, meaning you could return to your current situation if your house hacking attempt does not work, with minimal loss. Rather than investing significant time and money into a new property to house hack, only to find out it is not the strategy for you, you can start slowly, with minimal risk.

Not only are you avoiding the risk of wasting your time and money on purchasing a new property by house hacking the property you currently own; you are also avoiding the risk of moving to a new home and/or area you do not like. If you really enjoy the current home and area you live in, a major concern you may have about house hacking is whether or not you will like the new property and area as much as your current one, or even at all. That risk is avoided by house hacking your current property.

If you currently own a property or have owned a property in the past, you know how time-consuming, stressful, and potentially costly a real estate transaction can be. If you had to sell your current property to purchase a new one specifically to house hack, you would have to go through the pain of a real estate transaction twice—once to sell your current property and once to purchase a new property. Since you can house hack the property you currently own, you can avoid both of those transactions.

ALERT

If you had to sell your current property to purchase another one, you could expect to pay between 2–6 percent in commission to your real estate agent for selling the property. Depending on the price of the property you're selling, that could be tens of thousands of dollars in commission alone.

Many people who own their house and are not house hacking find it difficult to save a significant amount of money each month after paying all their expenses. If you think back to the discussion in Chapter 1 about the mortgage approval process, this should not come as a surprise, and that may even describe your current situation. Because of this, someone who already owns a home may find it difficult to save up enough money for a down payment on a new property to begin house hacking. A benefit of house hacking your current home is that it can remove you from this paycheck-to-paycheck cycle, as you do not have to save money for a new down payment and to cover closing costs.

Reducing or Eliminating Your Largest Expense

According to a report released by the US Bureau of Labor Statistics, the largest category of spending for the average American is housing, at 33.1 percent of their pretax income. It is not close, either. Housing costs are the largest category by more than two times the second-largest category, transportation. If you were to look at this data on an after-tax basis, the percentage of housing costs would be even higher.

FACT

The top three spending categories for the average American are housing, transportation, and food. On average, Americans spend 33.1 percent of their pretax income on housing, 15.9 percent on transportation, and 12.9 percent on food.

The key takeaway from this data is not the percentages themselves, as those will change from person to person and location to location, but rather the relationship between housing costs and income. The overarching problem is that many individuals do not have enough money left over after paying their bills to do the things they are passionate about or to save.

Let's look at a possible real-world scenario for someone following the traditional homeowner path to understand how having such a high percentage of income going toward housing costs is limiting. Assuming your annual income is $60,000, which is just about the annual average in the United States, you would earn $5,000 per month before taxes. After paying approximately 20 percent in income taxes, you are left with $4,000. The average annual housing cost for an American earning $60,000 is $19,884, or $1,657 per month, which is 33.1 percent of their pretax income. When considered on an after-tax basis, housing costs jump to 41.4 percent of income. This leaves you with $2,343, of your original $4,000, to pay the rest of your bills. After covering your student loans, auto loan, food, retirement savings, healthcare, and other expenses, you likely are not left with much each month to save.

Because you are unable to save, you are stuck playing defense rather than offense. This is one of the most overlooked concepts when it comes to personal finance and investing. You have probably heard the saying about the rich getting richer, right? When people hear this expression, they nod their heads in agreement, without giving it much more thought than their initial surface-level reaction. In a sense, that saying is true, but what it really means is that the rich are able to go on offense. They can take advantage of opportunities; they are not stuck playing defense. It is very difficult, if not impossible, to build wealth while being stuck on defense.

If you make $60,000 per year, you probably can't go on offense in the same way someone who is truly rich can. However, the same principle can be applied, just on a smaller scale. For the everyday person, going on offense can look like taking a job opportunity that is better in the long run but tougher in the short run. If you were offered a new job at a startup making $45,000–$50,000, even if you knew the company had strong prospects and was going to be successful—meaning you would have an opportunity to advance and be given stock options—you still could not accept the position with your current financial situation. You are stuck on defense. Even though your new position could pay from $75,000 to $100,000 or more annually over the next one to three years, plus potentially hundreds of thousands of dollars in stock options, you cannot take the leap by leaving your current job for your new opportunity. You simply could not afford your lifestyle. You cannot go on offense.

By house hacking, you can reduce or eliminate your largest expense and go on offense. House hacking itself can generate significant wealth for you, but it is the additional opportunities that house hacking opens up to you that assist in making you truly wealthy.

Starting Without a Lot of Money

When it comes to real estate, there is a common misconception that you need to be a millionaire, or at least have a lot of money, to invest in real estate. Many assume it takes $50,000 to $100,000-plus in cash to start investing in real estate. Decades ago, maybe that was true. Even today, in some deals, that can be true. But it certainly is not the only way.

This misconception is born from two things. The first is the assumption that real estate investing means buying large apartment buildings or flipping run-down properties, which can take a lot of cash. The second is that the commonly touted loan structure for investment properties of 20–25 percent down is the only option to acquire real estate investments. Investing in apartment buildings or flipping properties is a real estate investing strategy you could pursue, and loan products with 20–25 percent down are also very common, but neither of these is the only option, and that is one of the biggest benefits of house hacking.

Because you are living in the property and claiming it as your primary residence, you can take advantage of financial products that require the property to be owner-occupied. Traditional investment properties are often considered to be riskier than owner-occupied properties, which is why loan products for traditional investment properties typically require a higher down payment percentage and almost always have a higher interest rate. While this can vary from institution to institution, and even deal to deal, investment property loan products typically require 20–25 percent as a down payment, with an interest rate of 1–2 percent higher than owner-occupied mortgages, and sometimes the loan term is required to be shorter. By house hacking, you can buy an investment property while still getting all the benefits of one of the best mortgage loan products available.

Instead of having to put 20–25 percent down, which is often a major barrier for many people, you have the opportunity to put potentially 0–5 percent down, depending on your qualifications. Let's assume you are going to purchase a $400,000 property. If you were purchasing this as a traditional investment property, you are most likely going to need between $80,000 and $100,000 just for the down payment, if not more. Whereas, if you purchase that *same* property as a house hack, you can put down between $0 and $20,000. While the upper end of that range is still a lot of money, $20,000 is a lot more attainable for most people than $80,000–$100,000.

You may be wondering how you can take advantage of the 0 percent down loan products. Unfortunately, they are not available to everyone, nor do they work in every situation, as they often have eligibility requirements for the borrower and/or the property itself. One of the most commonly known and used 0 percent down loan products is the VA (Veterans Affairs) loan. If you or your co-borrower fits the eligibility requirements for VA loans, this can be one of the best ways to purchase a house hack and make the already-great benefits of house hacking even better.

There are other, lesser-known loan products that require 0 percent down as well. Similar to VA loans, there are eligibility requirements that must be met in order to use the loan product, but for those who qualify, they can be great resources. Surprising to most, there is a 0 percent down loan product offered through the US Department of Agriculture (USDA). Both the VA loan and loans offered through the USDA program are typically used by traditional home buyers. However, one of the largest benefits of house hacking is that you are also able to take advantage of these loan products.

ESSENTIAL

For readers who are even more creative, there are other financial products or strategies, such as 203k loans, HomeReady or Home Possible programs, a home equity line of credit (HELOC), private capital, hard money loans, seller financing, or even partnering with someone who also wants to house hack.

When You're Ready to Move On

Just being able to take advantage of the low down payment and low-interest loan products that were just discussed is a major benefit of house hacking, but the benefits improve when you dig a bit deeper. Because you are occupying the property as your primary residence, you can take advantage of the best loan products—but how long do you have to live in the property?

Are you required to stay there forever to take advantage of these loan products? Do you have to refinance to a different type of mortgage when you move out?

Typically, you are only required to maintain that property as your primary residence for one year after getting the mortgage. Then you can move out and do as you wish with the property, without having to refinance to a different type of mortgage. You are required to maintain that property as your primary residence for a year, but that does not mean you cannot sell the property within a year. If you choose to sell it less than twelve months after purchasing it, that is typically not a violation of your loan agreement. You just cannot purchase another property within twelve months with an owner-occupied loan product and claim it as your primary residence. You cannot have two primary residences.

ALERT

There is nuance with Federal Housing Administration (FHA) mortgages, whereby you cannot have two FHA loans at the same time. This means if you used an FHA loan to buy a house hack, you can't use an FHA loan for your next property as long as you still actively have the initial FHA loan. Be sure to discuss the details of your loan product with your lender.

Once you have lived in the property for one year, you have several options for moving forward with the property. You can sell it, choose to no longer house hack, and buy your forever home. You could keep the property as a rental property but still decide to not house hack again, or you can use the money you were able to save while house hacking to house hack again. The flexibility to exit a house hack is certainly a big benefit of this strategy. It makes it an asymmetric bet—you have large potential upside with minimal, or capped, downside risk. But the real benefit of house hacking comes from when you continue to house hack, over and over.

Shortening Time to Financial Freedom

What if you could retire or achieve financial freedom in three to five years just from house hacking? This is one of the biggest benefits of house hacking—it can dramatically shorten the amount of time it takes for you to achieve financial freedom.

One of the most common properties used to house hack is a duplex, so this property type will be used to illustrate exactly how house hacking can shorten your time to financial freedom. Once you have learned how the process and numbers work with a duplex, you can extrapolate that over more units, such as a triplex or a fourplex, and also use it to fit your exact income and purchase price situations.

As an example, let's assume you purchase a two-bedroom, one-bath duplex for $350,000 with the intention of house hacking. You will live in one unit and rent out the other one. Market rents in this area are about $1,500 per month for two-bedroom, one-bath units. Your all-in cost for your mortgage is $2,000 per month, including principal, interest, taxes, insurance, and PMI. While you live in one of the units, your portion of the mortgage is $500 per month, since you will be receiving $1,500 in rent. Remember how you learned that house hacking reduces your largest expense—your living costs? This arrangement allows you to live for $500 per month in the same house as someone who is paying $1,500 per month. Being able to do this saves you $1,000 per month that can be put toward saving, investing, or even splurging here and there.

> **FACT**
>
> Total monthly rental income minus mortgage expense equals gross profit. Reserves should be set aside from the monthly gross profit to cover maintenance, repairs, and capital expenditures (CAPEX) when those issues arise.

Now let's say that you have lived in the property for more than twelve months and decided you enjoyed house hacking, especially living so cheaply, but you are ready to move on to another property. Instead of selling the duplex you currently live in, you rent out your unit at the same market rent as the other unit, $1,500 per month, and now collect $3,000 per month in total monthly rental income. Your mortgage is approximately $2,000 total, so you now have a gross profit of $1,000 per month.

If you remember, the average American makes about $60,000 annually. This equates to approximately $4,000 per month on an after-tax basis. You can use a simple calculation to back into how many duplexes are needed to replace your current income. If you earn $4,000 per month, that can be replaced by just four duplexes that have a monthly gross profit of $1,000 per month. To perform this calculation for your income and gross profit, calculate your monthly net income and divide it by your rental property's total monthly gross profit. The resulting number tells you how many of those properties you would need to replace your income.

There can be nuances to this calculation when you consider the benefits your employer may provide, such as a 401(k) and health insurance, as well as taxes and property repairs, but the idea is the same. A few high-quality house hacks can significantly shorten the time it will take you to achieve financial freedom.

ESSENTIAL

Not all of the properties you purchase to house hack will have the same gross profit number, even if they are the same property type. Changes in market rents, financing terms, and purchase price can cause your gross profit number to vary, even across properties that are nearly identical.

Since you are only required to maintain a property as your primary residence for twelve months when using an owner-occupied loan, you can repeat this process nearly every year. If you are twenty-five years old, that means you could be financially free by thirty. If you are thirty, it means you could be financially free by thirty-five. No matter your age, this strategy means you could reach financial freedom in five years.

If you are paying rent or mortgage of $1,500 per month and living on what you have left, when you can reduce that expense to $500 per month through house hacking, you can put $1,000 savings aside each month as you work toward your next house hack. At the end of the year, the $12,000 you saved is enough for a 3.5 percent down payment on a $340,000 house. By repeating your steps, you could realistically do this every twelve months. Even if you need an extra three to six months to save more than $12,000 to buy your next house hack, completing this process every fifteen to eighteen months would still significantly reduce the amount of time it would take you to achieve financial freedom.

A common approach to achieving financial freedom and/or early retirement is to save enough in your retirement accounts, such as 401(k)s and IRAs, to be able to withdraw a portion each year and fund your lifestyle. A generally accepted amount for a safe withdrawal rate is 4 percent. Assuming a 4 percent withdrawal rate each year and not having to pay taxes on your withdrawals, you would need to save $1,200,000 in your retirement accounts to replace your after-tax income of $4,000 per month. You would need $1,500,000 in your retirement accounts to replace your pretax income of $5,000 per month.

QUESTION

How long would it take you to save $1.2–$1.5 million?
You would need to save $250 per month for forty-five years at an 8 percent rate of return to save $1.2 million, and about forty-eight years to save $1.5 million.

The timeline given in Chapter 1 to achieve financial freedom by investing in the stock market fits perfectly into the common retirement narrative. Most people begin working around the age of twenty to twenty-two, work and save for forty-five years or so, then retire around sixty-five. While there is nothing inherently wrong with this, and many generations have followed this model, there has been a massive growing disdain toward this approach to retirement. Recent generations are no longer willing to spend their entire lives working in order to enjoy a much shorter time in retirement.

If you would like five house hacks at $1,000 per month in gross profit to cover your $4,000 per month after-tax income, to ensure you have enough extra income per month to cover the lost benefits from your employer and taxes, and you only house hack every eighteen months instead of every twelve months, it would still only take seven and a half years to achieve financial freedom. That is far, far less time than the forty-five-year timeline of investing exclusively in retirement accounts.

There are two important points regarding the two approaches toward financial freedom. The first is that when house hacking, you are not required to quit your job just because you hit your mark for financial freedom. If you have house hacked enough to replace your income but you would like to keep working, that is absolutely an option! The second is the level of income in retirement. In the retirement accounts strategy, you are limiting yourself to the same level of income and lifestyle in your retirement years that you currently have. The markets could outperform the 7 percent rate of return used in the calculation, which would provide you more income, but that is completely out of your control. Whereas with house hacking, if you decided you wanted more income, you could simply purchase another house hack or even a traditional rental property. You can also go on offense. You can take advantage of other, more risky opportunities that can significantly increase your income that you may not have been able to before.

While house hacking may not always be glamorous, and you will almost certainly need to make sacrifices for a period, consider the alternatives. Would you rather make sacrifices for three to eight years and live the rest of your life in financial freedom, or would you rather live a more typical lifestyle and postpone retirement until your sixties?

Being able to shorten the amount of time it will take you to achieve financial freedom in a low-risk, proven way is a major benefit of house hacking.

Flexibility with Your Lifestyle

You just learned quite a bit about how house hacking can shorten the amount of time it will take you to achieve financial freedom, but what if you are not in a rush to achieve financial freedom? What if you are one of the lucky ones that truly enjoys your work and has no intention of stopping anytime soon?

House hacking does not require you to quit your job. You do not have to *actually* retire as soon as you hit your financial freedom number. You have the option to do that if you so choose, but you do not have to. Instead, what you would have is fantastic flexibility.

You could go on offense by taking advantage of an awesome career opportunity you otherwise would not have been able to. An opportunity becomes available at a new, exciting startup that is working on a product or mission you are very passionate about—you have the flexibility to go on offense and give it a shot. The flexibility and security that allowed you to take the risk, oddly enough, can lead to even more flexibility and security when you are successful. The process can be self-fulfilling.

Your boss won't approve your time-off request for something that is really important to you? You can do it anyway because you are not worried about the potential repercussions. You have taken control and will have the flexibility to pursue other jobs that will not put you in that situation. Maybe it is not just a time-off request; maybe it is a toxic boss, coworker, or corporate culture. Whatever the negative situation is that is not allowing you to be happy with your work, you will have the flexibility to go elsewhere and find true enjoyment in your work.

Flexibility with work is a great benefit of house hacking, but it also provides flexibility in other aspects of your life. You have probably heard the term "house poor." This refers to purchasing a home that requires a significant portion of one's income, leaving them little money for anything else. This commonly occurs during the traditional process of purchasing a home, which you learned about in Chapter 1.

On one hand, it is understandable to want to buy a house that you really love. After all, you spend a significant amount of time there. But is it worth it if you are unable to do other things you enjoy? Would you be happier if you spent less money on your housing costs so you could do other things? Instead of having to skip out on an amazing girls'/guys' trip or postponing that dream vacation, wouldn't it be worth taking an untraditional approach to homeownership if it meant you could participate in those activities?

What if you never had to miss one of your child's events—a soccer game, dance recital, or school play? Would that be worth it?

A benefit of house hacking is that it gives you a lot of flexibility in your life. It provides you flexibility with your job, it enables you to travel more, it allows you to spend more money and time doing the things you truly enjoy, and it can even reduce your stress and guilt.

Learning with Training Wheels On

There are some misconceptions around the difficulty of managing investment properties and the experience required to do so. Many aspiring real estate investors worry that they don't know enough or don't have enough experience to get started. Understandably, it can be daunting to manage rental properties without ever having done it before.

ALERT

Rental property experience and knowledge are applicable and are often discussed in the context of house hacking because the units or rooms the owner is renting operate very similarly to a traditional rental.

House hacking can solve this inexperience problem. A benefit of house hacking is that it allows you to learn and gain experience in a low-risk, easier way. For that reason, house hacking is often referred to as learning with training wheels on or "landlording-lite."

Rather than jumping into trying to purchase and manage an apartment building, you can learn on a smaller scale with more control. All the different strategies of house hacking will be discussed in the next two chapters, but the most common situations include a single-family home where bedrooms or a basement are rented, or a duplex where one unit is rented and the other is occupied by the owner. In both of these cases, you're starting on a much smaller scale and can learn at an easier pace.

With an apartment building, you're not only managing potentially dozens to hundreds of tenants; you're also handling any maintenance, repair, or CAPEX issues that may arise from all of those units. With a house hack, the most complex situation would be with three rental units in a fourplex or three to four roommates in a rent-by-the-room situation in a single-family home.

Some investors will argue that being local to your properties is not necessary and could even be a hindrance. The reason for this is that when you live close to your investment properties, you may be inclined to visit them whenever there is an issue, rather than using a team member to solve the problem, which leads to you working *in* your business rather than *on* your business. This is the opposite of what most investors want to actually do. However, many new investors find comfort in being near their properties, especially at the beginning. You can't get much closer or have more access to your investment properties than you do when house hacking.

Receiving Tax Benefits from Your Primary Residence

When someone begins to research personal finance and tries to take control of their money, they generally look at two areas—income and expenses. There are two ways to increase how much money you're able to save or enjoy, and those are to increase your income or decrease your expenses. When it comes to expenses, people often look at how much they're spending on food, going out, shopping, and so on, but what is often missed and not considered is how much they're paying in taxes.

This is a psychological phenomenon that occurs because people typically do not see the amount of money they're paying in taxes, like they do when they buy groceries or go out to dinner. Of course, that information is readily available on their paystubs, but with the prevalence of direct deposit, not many people ever see it. It is like that old saying: "out of sight, out of mind." Because of this, many financial professionals and educators highly recommend automating your saving and investing.

If this process happens automatically, the amount you receive each pay period, net of savings and investing, becomes normal, and you learn to live off that amount. It works the same way with taxes, despite it being the largest expense for many people. At first, the amount you are automatically saving is noticed since it reduces what you have remaining, but after a relatively short period of time, the amount you have remaining becomes your new baseline and you almost forget your previous baseline. This psychological phenomenon is hedonic adaptation, which says that humans revert to a new baseline, whether due to a positive or negative change, relatively quickly. It works the same way with new cars and material items too. At first, your fancy new car seems great, but then hedonic adaptation kicks in and your fancy new car simply becomes your new baseline and you are unlikely to be any happier than you were with your old car, or your old baseline.

ESSENTIAL

You do not need to be a tax expert to be a successful house hacker, but at least understanding the fantastic tax benefits from even a basic level that house hacking can provide adds another exceptional advantage to the house hacking strategy.

A major benefit of house hacking is that it can help reduce your annual tax bill. It probably will not reduce the amount taken automatically from your paycheck each pay period, but it can have an impact on how much you pay in taxes at year end, which can still be a substantial savings. When you purchase a property as a traditional homeowner, you have very few items that are tax deductible or creative tax options. However, when you purchase a house hack, that becomes a business, which opens up the world of tax options for you. As a house hacker, you can deduct expenses related to running your rental units, take advantage of depreciation, and even use the two-out-of-five-year rule, or 1031 exchange. These concepts will be discussed in more detail in Chapter 12.

CHAPTER 3

Conventional Strategies of House Hacking

Some investing strategies are defined and lack flexibility. House hacking is just about the complete opposite. There are nearly endless possibilities with house hacking; the only limitation is your imagination. Regardless of your situation, there is a sub-strategy of house hacking that can work for you. Some of the strategies are a bit more conventional, while others take a bit more imagination. If you're willing to open your mind, put in some hard work, and make a few sacrifices, there is a house hacking strategy for you. In this chapter, you'll learn how to house hack the more conventional ways, using multifamily properties, accessory dwelling units (ADUs), and single-family properties.

Multifamily Properties and ADUs

The strategy of house hacking can take shape in many ways. Broken down into its simplest form, house hacking is simply renting out additional space in a property you own that you are not using. In this chapter and the next, you will learn some of the most conventional, and unconventional, strategies you can implement to do just that.

Most people think of multifamily properties and ADUs when they learn about house hacking for the first time. House hacking using a multifamily property is when you purchase a two- to four-unit property, live in one of the units, and rent out the others.

Multifamily Properties

The term "multifamily" has a broad meaning in the real estate industry because it can include properties with two units (a duplex) all the way up to apartment buildings with hundreds of units. To delineate between these different types of multifamily properties, those with four units or fewer will be considered small multifamily.

ESSENTIAL

Multifamily properties with five units or more are considered commercial real estate in the eyes of a lender. Instead of working with a traditional mortgage lender and underwriter, you would be rerouted to the commercial lending department. There are different loan products and programs for commercial loans, so it is essential to understand the difference and cutoff between noncommercial and commercial multifamily real estate.

There are no requirements as to what the units must consist of in a small multifamily property in terms of bedrooms or bathrooms or even which unit the owner must live in. The owner just has to live in one of the units in the property to satisfy the loan requirements. Some multifamily properties may have identical units, or they may all be different. If the units are different and one is significantly nicer and/or bigger than the other(s), the owner can choose to live in that unit. However, there is a business decision that must be made before making that final decision, because the bigger, nicer units will usually bring in more rental income. You may need to make a sacrifice by not living in the nicest unit if you want to reduce your living expenses as much as possible with that property.

ADU

An accessory dwelling unit, also known as an ADU, is simply a housing unit that is secondary to the main living space. An ADU could fall under the categories of multifamily or single-family finished basements. There are many different types of ADUs, such as attic space conversions, garage conversions, basement conversions, detached, or additions. Some ADUs, such as garages and detached, are completely separate structures from the primary property, while others are attached or part of the primary property. An ADU is similar to a separate unit in a small multifamily property in that it typically has its own kitchen, bathroom, and living area(s).

For the ADU to be legal, the property owner must have permits for building it. If you purchase a property with an already-established ADU, be sure that the correct permitting has been completed. You do not want to purchase a property that you thought had a legal ADU only to find out later that it was not actually built legally. At that point, it will most likely be your problem, not the previous owner's.

> **ALERT**
>
> There are local state and city ordinances that determine what is permitted or prohibited for ADUs. Some states and cities allow attached ADUs in all zoning districts where single-family homes are permitted, while others may be a bit stricter with their requirements. Be sure to check with your local government agency/office in charge of zoning and housing.

A great benefit of ADUs is that they can provide the opportunity to house hack if you have not been able to otherwise with a given property. If you were interested in house hacking but just could not find a multifamily property in your area, you could build an ADU in a single-family home, as long as it is permitted by your city. As the property owner, you could live in the ADU and rent out the rest of the house, or you could live in the house and rent out the ADU. The former is likely less comfortable for you than the latter, but it is almost guaranteed to be much more profitable. You could also do a mix of both, where you live in the house while the ADU is being built, then you move into the ADU for the remaining months until you hit your twelve-month requirement from your loan, and then you could move out of the property altogether.

To house hack with an ADU, you do not have to build an entirely new structure. Depending on the characteristics of the property you are going to purchase, you may be able to just finish an area that is currently unfinished to convert it into an ADU. You could finish the attic space above the garage, the garage itself, or even the basement.

FACT

In real estate, "finishing" a space is making changes to an area that was previously inhabitable so that it is habitable. Unfinished spaces are often usable for storage and other purposes, but they lack the amenities required to be livable. After an area is finished, it is ready to be inhabited.

The Benefits of These Properties

House hacking with multifamily properties and ADUs presents the fewest drawbacks compared with other strategies. The largest drawback is that you are living close to or next to someone else. For those who have only lived in a single-family property, this may be a new dynamic. For those who have lived in apartments or multifamily properties, this may not be a drawback—it may even be an improvement. When purchasing a multifamily property or a property with an ADU, you are in control of what that experience is like. If you see it as a drawback, you can control to what extent you allow it to be a disadvantage. Multifamily properties and ADUs provide a lot of flexibility when house hacking, but this is truly just the tip of the iceberg of the possibilities and flexibility that are available when house hacking.

Single-Family Finished Basements

Many people assume that renting out space in a property means a separate unit from where the owner is living, but that does not have to be the case. Some of the ADUs that were just discussed are separate from the owner's living space, but some are not. Another house hacking strategy is renting a finished basement in a single-family house.

You might recall that basement conversions were previously listed as an option for ADUs. However, this example differs from that. A legal ADU has a separate kitchen, bathroom, and living area from the main property. That *could* fall under the single-family finished basements category, but this is different. Renting a single-family finished basement that is not an ADU would be providing an area that is habitable but may not have all the necessities to be considered an ADU. For example, a finished basement may not include a kitchen or bathroom, in which it would not be considered an ADU, but you could still rent out the basement as its own "unit." There would need to be an understanding with the tenants of what is and is not included, and you likely would not be able to demand market rents.

> **ALERT**
>
> Another potential downside to finishing your basement is that you will likely have to cover the costs with your own cash. If you have equity in the home, you may be able to tap in to that to fund the renovations, but if you just recently purchased the property, that may not be an option.

Similar to ADUs, this strategy allows you the opportunity to house hack if you cannot do so with the property you have selected. One of the main goals of house hacking is to reduce your living costs, which this strategy will allow you to do. However, one of the downsides of this approach is that you will not be able to use the income generated by the finished basement to qualify for the loan to purchase the property.

When you purchase a multifamily property, the loan underwriter decisioning your loan application will usually add a percentage of the potential income from the rental units to your income to help you qualify for the loan. Each lender can be different, but typically lenders will use anywhere from 70 to 90 percent of the rental income generated from a property toward your loan qualification.

ESSENTIAL

There is no specific rule or law that lenders must follow when accepting potential rental income. Lenders can differ in terms of how much rental income they will accept in their underwriting process. If you ask your mortgage processor, they should be able to tell you exactly what percentage of rental income they use.

If you are purchasing a fourplex and the three rental units have a market rent of $1,000 each, the loan officer would add those three together ($3,000), take 70–90 percent of that ($2,100–$2,700), and add it to your income on your loan application. This is for small multifamily properties only and is not done for single-family properties. This does *not* mean that you cannot use a single-family house to house hack, nor does it mean you will not qualify for the loan; it simply means that you cannot use the rental unit(s) income to purchase a property that you would not qualify for with only your income.

FACT

If you are acquiring a property without existing tenants, lenders will find comparable rental rates in your property's area, known as rental comps, and use those values for underwriting, similar to how appraisals are done to determine the value of a property using comps, or comparable sales. If there is already a lease in place, that is often used instead.

Single-Family Rent-by-the-Room

If the basement is not considered an ADU but is still finished and rented out to tenants, you could rent it under the single-family rent-by-the-room category. However, this strategy specifically relates to a more traditional sense of "bedrooms." This means you purchase a three- or four-bedroom single-family house, live in one of the bedrooms, and rent out the others. A basement area is a bit more separated and secluded, whereas the bedrooms are typically all quite similar and closer together.

The financing drawback mentioned previously in the single-family finished basement category holds true here as well. This will be the case nearly anytime you purchase a property with only one legal unit, regardless of the strategy you employ after the acquisition. The strategy you implement and the income it generates helps you reduce your personal living expenses, but it cannot help you qualify to purchase the property.

> **ALERT**
>
> Even though you are sharing the space with your tenants, do not forget to draw up a lease! If you were to rent an apartment with roommates, the landlord or apartment building owner would make you all sign the lease. It's the same situation, but now you are the landlord.

If this strategy were plotted on a comfort versus profitability graph, with comfortability on the x-axis and profitability on the y-axis, that illustrates the dynamic between the amount of comfort given up versus the amount of profit you can earn, you would see it toward the top right of the graph. You have to give up the most comfort of any strategy, since you are living with roommates and sharing a bathroom and kitchen, but it is also one of the most profitable strategies. You can learn more about the relationship between comfortability and profitability when implementing any of the house hacking strategies discussed in this book at https://everythinghousehacking.com/comfort-versus-profits.

Let's look at an example of how this strategy's profit may be different than other strategies. You go the multifamily house hacking route and purchase a two-bedroom, one-bathroom duplex for $350,000, with a total monthly payment of $2,000, including principal, interest, taxes, insurance, and PMI. You rent out one of the units for $1,300, and you live in the other unit. This is a great success—rather than renting and paying the market rent of $1,300 per month, you can cut that nearly in half and live for only $700 per month! You have an extra $600 per month to save, invest, or spend, all while not having to sacrifice much comfort.

However, instead of going that route, let's say you sacrifice a bit more comfort and buy a single-family property and go with the rent-by-the-room strategy. Since you are only buying one house, instead of essentially two with a duplex, you find a four-bedroom, one-and-a-half-bathroom single-family property for $350,000. This keeps your total monthly payment at $2,000, including principal, interest, taxes, insurance, and PMI. You rent out three of the bedrooms and live in the remaining one. The market rent in your area for a studio or one-bedroom apartment is between $800 and $950. Since those scenarios allow for the renter to live alone, whereas your house does not, you provide a discount and rent each room for $700 per month. Using the rent-by-the-room strategy, you are bringing in $2,100 in monthly rent. Therefore, you are making $100 in profit over your mortgage payment each month. Instead of paying hundreds or thousands of dollars each month for rent or mortgage, you are essentially getting paid to house hack.

ESSENTIAL

It can sometimes be difficult to know exactly what to charge for rent in a rent-by-the-room situation. Providing a small discount to the market rate for studio or one-bedroom apartments is typically a good starting point. You can and should always adjust the rate based on the demand you receive and input from the market.

The multifamily house hack example is significantly better than the traditional path of homeownership because you can reduce your expenses by

$600 per month while building equity and taking advantage of tax benefits. However, you are quite far to the left on the hypothetical comfort versus profitability graph because you are not sacrificing much comfort and therefore you are sacrificing some profitability. Whereas the rent-by-the-room strategy sacrifices more comfort in order to gain more profit.

Bonus Rent-by-the-Room

Many of these strategies can be mixed and matched. You can choose to do only one, but you could also do several at the same time. For example, instead of house hacking a multifamily property or a single-family house to rent by the room, you could buy a multifamily property *and* employ the rent-by-the-room strategy. Instead of renting out the second unit in a duplex to just one tenant for $1,300 per month, you could rent it out to two tenants via the rent-by-the-room strategy and collect $1,400 per month. If you really wanted to supercharge this strategy, you could *also* rent out your unit using the rent-by-the-room strategy. Since your unit is also two bedrooms, you could live in one bedroom and rent out the other for $700 per month. Now you are bringing in $2,100 in rent each month, instead of the $1,300 you would be with the multifamily house hacking strategy.

Live-In Flips

Live-in flips may be the least conventional strategy discussed in this chapter, but they are still quite common, and many people use this strategy without even realizing it.

A live-in flip is a house hacking strategy where you purchase a property that is not in perfect condition, but it is livable. You renovate the property while living there, and then sell or rent the property when you decide to move out. When you purchase a property to complete a live-in flip, there will probably need to be maintenance, repairs, or renovations, but you will be able to live there safely without much hindrance to your daily life—it just may not be up to your standards yet. While you live there, the renovations are completed, the property is brought up to your standards, and you are gaining equity through forced appreciation. The homeowner often does this work because they are living there and it might be easier to complete weekend projects instead of hiring a contractor, but you can complete a valid live-in flip without ever lifting a hammer by hiring out the work to contractors.

ESSENTIAL

When most people think of flipping a property, they envision a massive rehab. In the case of a live-in flip, it can be a large rehab, but it can also be relatively minor and still work for this strategy. Live-in flips often involve landscaping projects, painting, replacing flooring, adding fixtures, and minor kitchen and bathroom remodels.

In the short term, the other house hacking strategies discussed in this chapter should reduce your monthly living costs if done correctly. However, a live-in flip does not accomplish this. Unless you are pairing a live-in flip with an aforementioned strategy, which you certainly can do, you are not collecting any rent, which means you are responsible for the entire mortgage and therefore not reducing your living expenses. There are benefits of the live-in flip strategy, like the other house hacking strategies; they just take a bit longer to realize as the investor.

In most house hacking strategies, you are benefiting from reduced living costs and also from natural appreciation of the property. The appreciation in these strategies comes from natural market appreciation rather than forced appreciation. Since appreciation is not being forced, there is less of it. With a live-in flip, you do not benefit from the reduced living costs, but you do likely benefit from greater appreciation. Instead of reducing your expenses a little bit each month, you get a bigger payout at the end.

One of the biggest drawbacks to the traditional real estate investing strategy of flipping is how heavily it is taxed. Since most properties are owned for only a short period and are an active strategy, the profits are taxed at some of the highest rates of any investing strategy. This means you lose a significant portion of your profit to taxes. A second drawback of traditional house flipping is that you also typically need significantly more capital, between 20–30 percent, to buy and renovate a property to flip.

A live-in flip solves both of these problems. As of this writing, the US tax code allows, for a single individual, the first $250,000 of capital gains to be completely tax-free if you have lived in a property for two of the last five years. If you are married, this amount jumps to $500,000. Depending on your personal tax situation, this can equate to a massive savings come tax time. Also, because you are purchasing the property as an owner-occupied property, and it is livable as is, you can still take advantage of the best mortgage products available for homeowners, which typically require between 3½ to 5 percent for a down payment. Similar to the other house hacking strategies discussed in this chapter, to satisfy the loan requirements, you only have to live in the property for one year. However, to take advantage of the tax benefits just described, you have to live in the property for two years instead of one.

ALERT

The US tax code that allows for tax-free capital gains is in the Section 121 exclusion and is often called the "home sale exclusion" or the "two-out-of-five-year rule." There are exceptions to this rule and frequent changes to the tax code, so be sure to consult with a tax professional for your specific situation.

The live-in flip strategy is interesting when considered on the hypothetical comfort versus profitability graph. In the short term, it would be quite far to the left because it requires little sacrifice of comfort and therefore garners little profit. As you move into the long term, you sacrifice a bit more comfort, as you have to live in a construction zone for a time, but you also gain significant profits from the forced appreciation.

No one of these strategies is particularly better than another. It all depends on which one is right for you. If you would like the cash flow each month to reduce your living expenses, then a multifamily or single-family rent-by-the-room strategy might be right for you. If you do not need the cash flow and would prefer the large appreciation on the back end, a live-in flip is the better choice for your situation. Of course, you must also consider the dynamic of comfort when picking your strategy. Some people are more willing to be uncomfortable in exchange for more profits than others. House hacking provides the flexibility; you just need to choose which strategy is right for you.

CHAPTER 4

Unconventional Strategies of House Hacking

Conventional house hacking strategies do require hard work and sacrifice, but they do not take much creativity. The strategies discussed in this chapter do require creativity, and a lot of it. If your friends and family do not think you are crazy for house hacking yet, they almost certainly will if, or when, you follow one of these strategies. If you truly want to find a way to house hack, there is a strategy out there for you. You may just need to get a little creative. In this chapter, you'll learn how to house hack in unconventional ways, using short-term rentals, vacation properties, and even RVs.

Short-Term Rentals (Airbnb/VRBO)

Airbnb has done such a great job marketing and making short-term rentals mainstream that its name is nearly synonymous with the entire concept of short-term rentals. Short-term rentals *did* exist long before Airbnb was created, but Airbnb, and similar platforms, like VRBO, have developed platforms that make the process far easier and more accessible to the masses. Regardless of what you call them, the strategy is the same. A property or space within a property is rented out to tenants for a period that is shorter than a standard lease. There is no firm definition of what exactly constitutes a short-term rental, but typically short-term stays are anywhere from one night to a couple of weeks. Stays longer than thirty days are usually considered to be traditional rentals.

ALERT

Many states and even cities have their own definition of what constitutes a short-term rental. They also often have laws and regulations about what is permitted or prohibited with short-term rentals in the area. Be sure to check your local laws and regulations before purchasing a property with a plan to use a short-term rental strategy.

There are a few ways you can incorporate short-term rentals into your property in order to house hack. The first strategy is to rent out the additional units in your multifamily property as a short-term rental instead of a long-term, traditional rental. In the previous chapter, you learned about multifamily and ADUs as a house hacking strategy. This is a similar approach, but instead of renting out the units you are not living in as traditional rental units, you can rent them as short-term rentals.

Before using this strategy, there are a few things you need to consider. The first is your estimated rental income from the short-term rentals. This can be hard to estimate, especially if you have no experience with short-term rentals. There are third-party platforms that provide short-term rental data that can assist you in calculating what you can expect for rental income from a short-term rental like yours in your area. To gauge what your rate may be, you can also check online short-term rental sites to see what other properties in your area are renting for.

To understand the level of demand, you can look at online reviews and availability of short-term rentals similar to yours in your area. If there are not many listings or few reviews for those that are listed, that may be an indicator that there is not much demand for short-term rentals in your area. However, if there are a lot of properties listed for rent and many of them have a lot of reviews, that could indicate there is strong demand in your area.

If you are still unsure or not confident in the data you have retrieved from these approaches, you can attend local real estate meetups and ask others what they know or what their experience has been. You can also speak with people who already have short-term rentals listed for rent in your area. Some of them may not be willing to speak with you, as you may be seen as competition, but there are likely to be at least a few people who have an abundance mindset and therefore would not mind sharing their experience.

It will also serve you well to do a bit of critical thinking on your own about the circumstances and area of your property. You may want to ask yourself a few questions that, when answered truthfully, may help you gain a clearer picture of what the short-term rental market might be like in your area. Do you live near an airport? Is the property in a vacation destination? Do people often travel there for business? Could people use this space as a place to stay when visiting a local college or university? Are there a lot of concerts or shows in town that people may need to stay over for? Does the area have a lot of hotels?

It is important to get a clear and confident understanding of what you can expect for rental income with short-term rentals before choosing that strategy over a traditional rental strategy. If you cannot confidently expect more rental income from short-term rentals than you know you can receive from traditional rentals, it is probably not worth it.

Why does the expected short-term rental income have to be significantly more than you would receive for a traditional rental? Why wouldn't one extra dollar be worth it? Because, with short-term rentals, you will have a lot more work than you would with traditional rentals, you will have increased costs, and you should build in a margin of safety.

There is inherently more tenant turnover with short-term rentals, which means more work. You will be handling booking requests, potential renters' messages and questions, multiple platforms' accounts, as well as cleaning the property and managing the rentals and any issues that arise, and more. You may be thinking, "But can't I hire a property manager?" You absolutely can, but there is still more work involved with managing a property manager, and that property manager management is more labor intensive for you as the owner of short-term rentals than of long-term rentals.

In addition to the increased effort, you will also likely have increased costs. If you ask any experienced residential real estate investor, they will probably tell you that one of the costliest aspects of owning rental properties is turnover. With short-term rentals, you have significantly more turnover. Now, the cost of turning over a short-term rental is probably less than a long-term rental, but it can still be costly, and *could* be similar to that of a long-term rental. Even with the best short-term renters, there is wear and tear on the rental unit with each stay, which adds up to items that need to be replaced over time. There are also platform and cleaning fees that reduce your profit. With a long-term rental, if the rent is $1,000 per month, you can expect to receive that amount each month; whereas, with a short-term rental, you will need to deduct a percentage of that $1,000 for the platform where you listed the property as well as for paying the cleaners.

> **FACT**
>
> "Margin of safety" is a term coined by Benjamin Graham that refers to adding a discount to the value you think something is worth so there is a buffer to help cover any mistakes you may have made in your calculations. Graham used this term in the context of stock investing, but it is a universal principle that could and should be applied to many types of investing

There is generally a higher degree of confidence in how much rent will be received each month with long-term rentals because of the ability to get comparable rental rates, a signed twelve-month lease, and the overall long-term nature of the rental. If someone signs a twelve-month lease for $1,000, you can estimate what you will receive in rental income over the next twelve months with more confidence than you could with a short-term rental. With short-term rentals, even when you are confident in your numbers, it is wise to add a margin of safety to your estimations. This will help provide a buffer if there are any errors in your calculation.

The size of your margin of safety is entirely dependent on your situation. If you know that short-term rentals are very popular in your area, you have done a lot of due diligence, and you are confident in your numbers, then you may be willing to use a lower margin of safety. If short-term rentals are less popular in your area or you are not overly confident, you will want to use a higher margin of safety. To add a margin of safety to your calculation, determine the percentage you would like to use, then remove that percentage from your estimated short-term rental profit. If you expect to earn $1,000 per month in short-term rental profit and want a 20 percent margin of safety, remove $200 (20% × $1,000) from your expected profit to make your new estimation $800 ($1,000 − $200).

It is important to add this margin of safety to your short-term rental profit and not just the rental income. If you add it only to your rental income, you are only adjusting for any miscalculations in the rental rate or demand. But if you add the margin of safety to your short-term rental profit as well, you are also adjusting for any miscalculations with your expenses such as platform fees, cleaning fees, maintenance, and repairs. Ultimately, estimating your profit is what is most important. If you can calculate your rental income correctly but you are off on the amount of money you get to actually keep, which is your profit, your rental income accuracy does not matter. Income is only half of the equation; you must accurately estimate your expenses as well.

If you estimate that you could earn $1,000 per month from a long-term rental in your multifamily rental unit, or $1,100 per month in profit if you used a short-term rental in that unit instead, would the extra $100 per month be worth all the effort, time, and risk of a short-term rental? This is not to say that it is *not* worth it, nor is it to say that this is a bad strategy. It can absolutely be worth it and be a great strategy; you just have to decide how much your profit would need to increase each month to cover the extra effort, time, and risk involved with a short-term rental versus a long-term rental. For some, $100 is enough. For others, the amount may need to be $500 or more. The strategy is available to you; the choice is ultimately yours.

Throughout this chapter, you have learned about renting the additional units in your multifamily property as short-term rentals instead of long-term rentals, but there are other ways to use short-term rentals as part of your house hacking strategy.

In Chapter 3, you learned about the rent-by-the-room strategy and a finished-basement strategy. Those were both assumed to be long-term tenants, but you can actually incorporate a short-term rental component into those strategies as well. Instead of renting out your spare bedrooms or basement to long-term tenants, you can rent them as short-term rentals. Most third-party short-term rental platforms allow property owners to designate whether the space listed is for an entire space or a room. You can select "room" or "shared space" and list your property for rent to short-term renters.

In addition to all the considerations you just learned about renting an additional unit as a short-term rental instead of a long-term rental, you also need to consider whether or not you, and other potential roommates, are comfortable with inviting strangers into your home while you live there. You can vet short-term renters before you accept them, but there is a difference between choosing a few people to live with long-term and having a revolving door of short-term renters. Some people are comfortable with this situation; others would never consider it. It is a strategy that is available to you—you do not *have* to use it.

> **ESSENTIAL**
>
> While short-term rentals have been around a while now, there are still changing laws and regulations across the world. Be sure to research how the area you want to buy in views short-term rentals and understand if there might be any legislation risk in the future.

Short-term rentals can also be used as part of your house hacking strategy by renting out your space when you are not using it. If you travel frequently or if you are going on a trip, you can list your space as a short-term rental. In this case, it is important to be cautious of your personal belongings and also the amount of time and effort it takes you to prepare your home for a short-term renter in comparison to what you receive in income. But this can provide you with a bit of additional income and even offset some of your travel expenses.

You can also mix and match other house hacking strategies with the short-term rentals strategy, creating many options. Maybe you have a triplex and want stable income from one of the units you do not live in, so you rent it on a long-term lease. Then, you rent the second unit you do not live in as a short-term rental to take advantage of the increased profitability that short-term rentals could provide and live by yourself in your unit. Maybe you go all-in on the short-term strategy by renting out the additional units as short-term rentals *and* short-term rental all the bedrooms in your house, except yours, of course. Maybe you use a mix-and-match strategy somewhere in between these two. The possibilities are limited only by your imagination.

RVs

Let's dive into how you might be able to use an RV to house hack. First, let's discuss what exactly an RV is and the different types that are available. RV stands for "recreational vehicle," and it can be thought of, in its simplest terms, as a house on wheels. There are many types within the overall category of RVs, such as Class A, Class B, Class C, travel trailers, fifth-wheel trailers, pop-up campers, and slide-ins. Class A, Class B, and Class C are all considered "drivables," while the rest are considered "towables."

The exterior of a Class A RV is similar to the buses that sports teams often travel in, with the interior of a home, including a bathroom, kitchen area, dining area, and sleeping space. Class B RVs are typically full-sized vans or cargo vans that have been remodeled inside to include living quarters. Class C RVs start with the frame of a typical pickup truck and add on a shell to replace the truck bed, which usually includes similar amenities to those of a Class A RV—bathroom, kitchen area, dining area, and sleeping space. All three of these RVs are considered drivables because they have their own engine and transmission that allow them to be driven under their own power.

Travel trailers and fifth-wheel trailers are very similar to the drivable RVs, except they do not have their own engine or transmission. As the category name implies, they must be towed by another vehicle. The biggest difference between the two trailers is the mechanism that is used to tow them. A travel trailer uses a traditional hitch system, whereas fifth-wheel trailers use a different system that is installed in the bed of a separate truck.

Pop-ups and slide-ins are similar to the travel trailers in that they do not have their own engine or transmissions and must be hauled by another vehicle, but they are different in their design. A pop-up folds within itself, similar to a tent, and travels all closed in, but it includes many of the amenities of other RVs when open. A slide-in is kind of like a do-it-yourself Class C RV. It consists of a shell, which includes living quarters, that is put in the back of a traditional pickup truck.

Now, how do RVs relate to house hacking? There are a few different ways. The first is that, if you have space in your driveway or yard, you can purchase an RV and rent it out as a short-term rental. You can think of this strategy as being similar to an ADU. The RV is essentially replicating a detached ADU. Instead of having to build the ADU, you purchased it. Your living costs, or mortgage, are offset by the income you receive by renting out the RV.

A benefit of this strategy is that you can house hack without having to share your space with someone else. They will be in your driveway or yard, but they will not be in your house or even attached to you. RVs also have good financing options that can help make this strategy profitable and can be used on your own. Cities and states often have laws and regulations for short-term rentals, ADUs, and sometimes even RVs. Be sure to check your local laws before pursuing this strategy.

ESSENTIAL

Before implementing this strategy, be sure to do the calculations necessary to ensure that the income from renting out the RV will at least cover the loan payment for the RV. If it does not, you are not house hacking. You would actually be going backward.

Another strategy you can use to house hack an RV is to stay in the RV yourself and rent your house or unit as a short-term rental. If you are in the first year of your mortgage, your house must remain as your primary residence, but you can spend periods of time staying in the RV. Be sure you fully understand the legal requirements of your mortgage and your city regulations so you do not unknowingly violate any of them.

You can choose to make your house available on short-term rental platforms for any possible day; that way you do not miss any potential listings. Then, if your house gets booked, you just stay in the RV for those days and nights. Similar to renting your house as a short-term rental when you travel, as discussed in a previous strategy, you can choose to make your house available if you are taking the RV on a trip.

You can also combine this strategy with other house hacking strategies. If you know you are going to be traveling, you can rent your house *and* the RV as short-term rentals. You could rent your spare unit as a long-term rental, your unit by the room as a short-term rental, and the RV as a short-term rental. There are nearly an endless number of combinations if you use your creativity. As with nearly all house hacking strategies, there is no right or wrong here. You can choose whichever option fits your lifestyle and goals best.

Vacation Properties

The strategy of house hacking vacation properties may be the most exciting and fun of all. However, it is also the least like true house hacking. In this book, this strategy is considered house hacking but not in the truest sense: You *are* house hacking; you are just not house hacking your primary residence. You are house hacking a vacation property.

Some people dream of having a vacation home somewhere tropical with fantastic beaches, others long for a home in the mountains where they can take advantage of the best skiing conditions, and others may want to be in a major city to enjoy all it has to offer. While the locations and goals of vacation houses may be different, there is one trait that is similar among these people and their situations—they think it's just a dream and unlikely to be achievable. They believe they must be rich to be able to own a vacation home. It takes hard work and some sacrifice, but by using a house hacking strategy, owning a vacation property is more attainable than you may imagine.

How exactly does house hacking a vacation property work? It is quite similar to the RV strategy discussed in the previous section, combined with a short-term rental strategy. To house hack a vacation property, you would purchase the property, rent it as a short-term rental when you are not planning on using it, and then stay in it whenever you choose. There is no right or wrong in terms of how much or when you choose to use the property yourself. However, depending on your choices, you may sacrifice some profitability.

As an example, if you chose a vacation property that is very popular during the Fourth of July in the United States, your short-term rental demand would be the strongest during that time. You would likely experience one of the highest rates for the year during that period. Therefore, if you use the property then instead of renting it out, you would be sacrificing a larger part of your potential profit than if you were to use it during an off-peak time.

> **ALERT**
>
> Other house hacking strategies in this book are hyperlocal; you share a property with someone. Vacation properties are often long-distance, which requires a few extra skills in addition to what is necessary for local investing. Using technology, investing long-distance is frequently done by investors, but it is something to be aware of going into this strategy.

With other house hacking strategies, there is the relationship between the amount of comfort given up and your potential profits. With the vacation property strategy, there is a similar dynamic, but with this relationship, the x-axis would become the number of days used. As the number of days increases, meaning you move right across the x-axis, your profitability would go down, meaning you move down the y-axis (learn more about this graph at https://everythinghousehacking.com/comfort-versus-profitability).

Not all days of you using the property are created equal, as illustrated in the Fourth of July example. Therefore, the steepness of the graph showing your actual situation may look slightly different, but the general relationship will remain the same. Theoretically, the more days you use, the less potential profitability you have. In your actual situation, if your "days used" number is increased by one on an off-peak day, you may not see the profitability data point drop much from the previous data. However, if your "days used" number increased by one on a peak day, you would see your profitability data point drop quite a bit from the previous data point.

In actuality, there will even be times when the profitability data point may not decrease at all as the "days used" amount increases. This would occur if you used the property on a day when you did not have it rented as a short-term rental because no one wanted to stay there. If there was a viable renter that you turned down so you could stay there, you would lose profitability, but if no one booked your property for certain days and you chose to use it because of that, you would not see a drop in your profitability data point on the chart. If you zoom out a bit on a graph showing your actual results, you would see that it very closely mimics that of the theoretical graph discussed, which shows that the more days you use, the less potential profit you have.

Similar to other house hacking strategies, this vacation property approach offsets your costs of using and enjoying the property yourself. Instead of buying a vacation house, letting it sit vacant when you are not using it, and paying a $2,000-per-month mortgage out of your own pocket, you can offset that mortgage each month with short-term rentals. If you purchase the right property in the right location, you may even be able to make a profit each month and only have a loss, or break even, in the months you use the property. Continuing with the example, rather than paying $2,000 each month, you could earn a monthly profit of, say, $1,000 for ten months out of the year for a total profit of $10,000, then use the property for the other two months. By house hacking a vacation property, rather than spending $24,000 per year on a mortgage, you are being *paid* $10,000 to enjoy your vacation house.

FACT

This house hacking strategy not only reduces the cost of the property itself; it can also reduce your overall travel expenses. The profit you earn from your vacation property can also be used to offset your travel costs to get to the property when you want to use it for your vacations.

In addition to the profits you may earn from the vacation property house hacking strategy, you also unlock tax benefits that would not have otherwise been available to you. Because your vacation property is now part of a business, you will likely have items that are tax deductible that would not be if you did not rent the property out. Depreciation, certain travel expenses, repairs, maintenance, and items for the house all may be at least partially tax deductible. The US tax code is ever-changing and nearly infinitely complex, so be sure to check in with your tax professional to understand the specifics of your tax situation.

Another benefit of using this strategy is that you may have access to better loan products than if you purchased the home as a traditional rental property. With many traditional rental property loan products, you need to put down 20–30 percent as a down payment. However, there are second home and vacation property loan products that only require a 10 percent down payment. Not only can the profits from renting it out make your vacation property more sustainable on an ongoing basis; the reduced down payment percentage also makes it more attainable up front. If you were to purchase a $400,000 property using a traditional investment loan product, you would be required to put down between $80,000 to $120,000 for the down payment, plus closing costs. With the second home loans, however, you would only be required to put down $40,000, plus closing costs.

As you learned in the Short-Term Rentals (Airbnb/VRBO) section earlier in this chapter, you need to do significant due diligence before purchasing a property and using it as a short-term rental. The same goes for house hacking a vacation property. If you can afford to cover the monthly mortgage payment every month for the next twenty or thirty years without any rental income, then you may not need to do as much due diligence. However, if you are going to be relying on the short-term rental income to cover a portion of the mortgage so you can afford the property, it is important to do significant due diligence up front. Just because you are purchasing the property as a vacation property and it is somewhere you would like to go for vacation, that does not mean other potential renters will necessarily agree. If others do not agree, there may not be a very strong short-term rental market. It is important to understand the rental market in the area you are looking to purchase in and what those numbers may look like for you.

CHAPTER 5

Your Real Estate Team

One of the most overlooked aspects of becoming a real estate investor is just how important relationships are to your success. From real estate agents to contractors to mentors—the relationship component is underappreciated. Being a real estate investor is considered an entrepreneurial venture, which people often think means it is an individual, "solopreneur" journey. This could not be further from the truth. There is the potential to succeed without a great team, but your odds of success are much higher with one. In this chapter, you'll learn what it means to have people on your team, as well as which people you need, their roles, and how to find them.

What Does It Mean to Be "On the Team"?

It can sound daunting when you hear you need to build a "team," especially if you have never done it before. Let's put those concerns to rest first, then you will learn who you need on your team and how you can find them.

Building a team does not mean you need to hire full-time employees, pay them a salary plus benefits, and offer them paid vacation. In fact, for the purposes of this book, it's not like that at all. For large apartment syndicators, your team can, and often does, include full-time employees, but with house hacking, it does not. Rather, you are building a group, or list, of real estate professionals that you have vetted and built relationships with ahead of time that you know you can rely on when you need their services. Best of all, they are generally not paid until their services are rendered—so no annual salary or up-front costs!

Whom Do You Need on Your Team?

A chain is only as strong as its weakest link. You have probably heard this saying in various aspects of life or business, but it can apply to your real estate team too. Each person on your team plays an important role that leads to your investing success. New investors often do not realize how much of a team sport real estate is, or how real estate is all about relationships. It is important to not only get members on your team but also to have the right members on your team.

When it comes to your team, its members can be broken down into three categories: pre-acquisition, post-acquisition, and administrative. Team members included in the pre-acquisition group are typically, but not exclusively, used during the pre-acquisition phase of purchasing a property. The professionals in the post-acquisition group are most commonly used after you've already acquired the property, and your administrative group can be used any time you need them. These three groups are broken down into the following professionals:

Pre-Acquisition

- Real Estate Agent
- Lender
- Inspector/Inspection Company
- Attorney
- Insurance Agent/Broker

Post-Acquisition

- Property Manager
- Handyman
- Electrician
- Plumber
- HVAC
- Carpenter
- Landscaper/Landscaping Company
- Locksmith

Administrative

- Virtual Assistant

QUESTION

Including an agent, I need fourteen people on my team just to buy one house hack?

Not quite. Not every person or every deal requires all fourteen of these people in order to successfully acquire and operate a house hack. If you invest in real estate long enough, you will probably need all of these people eventually, but in the beginning, it's valuable to at least understand who these people are, why they're important for your team, and how to find them.

Team Member Roles and How to Find Them

There is a common debate in the real estate world that some real estate agents are or aren't worth the seemingly large commissions they *can* earn. If you find a subpar agent who doesn't provide much value, you may argue the latter point. If you work with a rock star real estate agent, as will be described throughout this chapter, you will likely fall into the group that argues for the former.

Not only do real estate agents play a pivotal role; they can arguably be the most important person on your team when used appropriately.

ESSENTIAL

In most real estate transactions, using an agent as a buyer comes at no cost to the buyer. The seller is paying a commission out of their proceeds to their agent, who then splits that commission with the buyer's agent. There can be exceptions, but this structure is the norm in most regular real estate transactions.

Real Estate Agent

Part of what makes a real estate agent effective is that they have a large list of vetted, trustworthy contacts they can recommend to you. You should always interview your agent's recommendations and verify they are up to your standards, but you will save a lot of time finding great team members by leveraging your real estate agent's network.

In addition to providing information about the best neighborhoods, having an invaluable list of contacts, and all of the other traditional tasks an agent does during the buying/selling process, your agent can help find tenants, offer showings to potential tenants, and, in some cases, even be your property manager.

If you plan to use a property manager, you may not need your real estate agent to do some of the tasks previously listed, but if you will not be using a property manager, the agents must be willing and able to complete at least those tasks. Typically, agents who have only worked with traditional buyers and sellers are not familiar with the level of increased effort required to work with an investor, nor are they aware of the additional tasks they'll be asked to do. These are not the types of agents you want to work with. You need an agent who has a successful track record of working with investors in the past, high-quality verifiable reviews online that you can check, and a list of references you can call. This last item isn't required, but it is a bonus if they're also a real estate investor.

Some investors may feel there is a conflict of interest when working with a real estate agent who is also an investor, because, by definition, they are looking for investments in the same area you are. However, the pros often outweigh the cons, and if they have a strong, verifiable track record of working with investors, you can feel confident that a high level of service will continue with you. Also, if you are looking for a house hack, you probably will not be in direct competition with your real estate agent—it's possible, but unlikely.

Following is a list of questions you can ask your potential real estate agent to help determine if they are a good fit for you:

- How long have you been a real estate agent? Why did you get into the business?
- Do you typically work with traditional home buyers and sellers, or do you frequently work with investors?
- Are you also a real estate investor? If so, which type of properties do you target? How many units do you own?
- Are you willing and able to submit a lot of offers on my behalf in a timely manner? It will likely take more offers for me to find a house hack than it does for a typical home buyer to purchase a primary residence—are you okay with that?
- If/when we get a property under contract, are you able to meet with the other real estate professionals that need to access the property (i.e., inspectors)?
- Do you offer property management services? If so, what is your rate? What tasks do you complete? If not, do you have a vetted, trustworthy

property manager/property management company that you can recommend?

- If I want to self-manage the property, are you willing and able to list the property for rent on my behalf, provide showings to potential tenants at the property, and complete the move-in/move-out condition report when a tenant is moving into or out of the property?
- Do you have and are you willing to provide a list of recommended real estate professionals that you have vetted and worked with in the past?
- Can you please provide a list of references, ideally three to five previous investor clients you've worked with in the past?

You are not required to ask all of the questions of every agent, nor are these the only questions you should ask. Rather, they provide a general idea of the types of questions you can ask, and you can, of course, add more questions. You should ask questions of the agents until you feel comfortable—no more, no less. If early in the conversation they state that they do not work with investors, you do not need to continue with your list of questions. You can politely end the conversation and continue on to your next topic.

You will want to start by leveraging platforms that offer reviews for agents, such as Zillow, Realtor.com, and Redfin, among others. In today's technology-driven world, it is recommended you work with agents who have an online presence and a verifiable track record of success and great customer service. As Newton's first law of motion says, "An object in motion stays in motion," and that likely holds true for real estate agents as well. If they have consistently received five-star reviews from previous clients, they will probably provide the same great service to you. The same can be said of negative reviews too; if they have consistently had bad experiences with clients in the past, that is likely to happen to you as well. Of course, there are exceptions to this rule, as there is with any rule, but this is a good place to start.

Once you've gathered a list of real estate agents with positive reviews, narrow that down to agents local to the area in which you're looking to purchase. If you're able to filter by characteristics, look for a category that states the agent actively works with investor clients. If this filter function or category isn't available, don't worry—you'll ask this question when you talk to the agent anyway. Once you've got a list of agents local to where you'd like to invest, start reading their bios and check out their websites and online profiles. Then, make a list of five to ten you'd feel comfortable working with based on their background and expertise. The last step is to interview the agents and pick one. Work your way through your list of agents by calling them, asking the previous questions as well as your own, and determining who is the best fit for you.

Keep in mind, this person will play a pivotal role in the success of your real estate investing, so take this part seriously. Make sure you're comfortable working with them, you've received and vetted references, they have the highest levels of integrity, are trustworthy, and you'd enjoy working with them. This last item is often overlooked by most investors, but it can completely change your experience.

ESSENTIAL

Abraham Lincoln once said, "Give me six hours to chop down a tree and I will spend the first four hours sharpening the axe." The idea behind this quote can be applied to real estate investing, and specifically to finding a real estate agent. There is certainly work necessary up front to find a good agent, but it is a worthwhile investment that makes the rest of your investing much, much easier.

Lender

Once you have found your go-to agent, the next person you'll need to add to your team is a lender. This is often a specific individual at a bank or mortgage company, like a loan officer or mortgage broker, but it doesn't have to be—it can be a company that you've built a relationship with. Often, it is best to work with banks or credit unions local to where you are purchasing, but it is not required. If you have a relationship with a bank/lender that is nationwide and you'd prefer to continue working with them, that is always an option.

It is important to build a relationship with a lender to ensure that you are aligned with their expectations. You do not want to go through the time and effort of finding a property and being ready to place an offer, only to find out you can't qualify for a loan which the deal depended on. Therefore, it is recommended you start working with a lender early in the process. What's helpful about starting the team-building process with an experienced real estate agent is that they should be able to recommend a lender. While the questions to ask potential agents listed in the previous section are optional, a list of vetted, trustworthy real estate professionals that they've worked with in the past and would highly recommend should be valued heavily. Therefore, you should ideally be able to get a recommended lender from your agent—if not more than one.

If your agent cannot provide a referral to a lender, that does not mean they can't be an effective agent, nor does it mean you can't find a lender—it just means you have to do a little more work yourself. Similar to the real estate agent process previously described, you should try to work with lenders that have a strong, positive online presence with a long track record of verifiable reviews. With all of the platforms available today, there are reviews for nearly every profession—use them.

Once you have recommendations from your agent or you've built a list of potential lenders, start calling them. Tell them your situation, where you live, what you're trying to do, the types of properties you're looking to buy, and your financial position. You'll want to ensure your situation is acceptable to them. For example, you'll need to meet their lending requirements, which you can usually find out without having a hard inquiry, an official request for credit, put on your credit report, and the properties you're looking at will need to be ones they'll agree to lend on. Some banks don't lend in certain areas, while others don't lend below a certain amount or on certain property types, so never assume that a bank will accept all aspects of your situation or deal—always call and verify.

Following is a list of questions you can ask your potential lender to help determine if they are a good fit for you:

- What are your income requirements?
- What is your job history requirement?
- What is your minimum credit score requirement?
- What is the minimum amount you'll lend for a mortgage? What is the maximum?
- What loan terms are available?
- Which loan products do you offer?
- Is it possible for my loan to be sold after closing? If so, do you retain servicing?
- How long does it generally take from application to closing, assuming no anomalies?
- Do you lend to LLCs (limited liability companies) or strictly to individuals?

Inspector/Inspection Company

A great inspector is generally the next person to add to your team, after you have an agent and lender. You can start calling around for an inspector whenever you feel comfortable, but it is generally best to wait until you have a property under contract. You can do this up front as you search for your property, but you run the risk of wasting your time and effort if you are not able to find a property or get one under contract.

Once a property is under contract, the next step is to get an inspection—if that is part of the contract. As soon as an agreement is reached to purchase a property, begin calling your potential inspectors, because there is generally a tight window for the inspection to be completed, and an inspector may not be able to come out right away. Contractors and inspectors are often in high demand and can be hard to get out to your property quickly.

You should leverage your real estate agent for their connections and referrals as much as possible. That goes for lenders, as were discussed previously; inspectors, as we're discussing now; and all the real estate professionals we'll discuss next. Your agent has probably worked with many inspectors in the past, so they should be able to point you in the right direction. If that is not an option, use a search engine like HomeAdvisor or a review site like Yelp. Both of these sites provide reviews for local professionals that you can use to vet potential candidates.

ALERT

Remember, reviews are a great place to start, but the search does not end there. Continue your due diligence and ask your questions—house hacking involves specific needs, so you need to ensure your needs can be met.

For example, you want an inspector that is thorough and trustworthy, and that will provide advice and guidance as if they were inspecting the property for their own purchase. You do not want someone that rushes through the inspection, doesn't pay attention to detail, and isn't willing to answer your questions.

Following is a list of questions you can ask your potential inspector to help determine if they are a good fit for you:

- How long have you been an inspector/in business?
- Have you worked with investors in the past? Any house hackers?
- Are you an investor yourself?

- Are you willing to treat this inspection as if you were inspecting a potential investment property for yourself?
- What are the major focal points of your inspection?
- What are typical issues you've noticed in properties in this area?
- Lacking construction skills, I will be relying heavily on your opinion to accurately access the current condition of this property. Are you willing to answer all of my questions regarding the inspection until I am comfortable and understand the status of the property?
- How often do you interject your opinion on what is considered a serious problem versus what is a minor, cosmetic issue?
- How long after the inspection is completed will the report be finalized?

Attorney

Unless you are a real estate attorney yourself, the legal paperwork involved in buying a real estate property can be a bit overwhelming. Buying real estate is often daunting enough for most people; you do not need to be weighed down by the pile of legal documents. You will want to have an experienced real estate attorney that is local to the area you're investing in to review the documentation throughout the transaction, as well as someone who is available if an issue arises once the transaction has closed. This not only gives you peace of mind on the front end; it also gives you a sense of security that you're protected into the future. However, you do not want a general attorney that is not focused on real estate or that is not local to the area. Having a real estate–specific attorney is important, and if you can find someone who specializes in house hacking and/or rentals, that's even better! It is also important that they're local to the area; that way they understand the intricacies and nuances of the local government organizations.

To find an attorney, you can get referrals from real estate agents, either the agent you have on your team or another agent in the area. Your agent should have an attorney that previous clients have used that they can refer you to, but if they do not, you can call other local real estate agents or brokerages and ask who they recommend. Similar to the other real estate professionals discussed, you can find reviews for attorneys on platforms like

Google Reviews or Yelp. However, there usually aren't a lot of reviews for attorneys on these platforms, so it can be difficult to gauge the quality of the attorney solely on that. The sample size is often just too small to draw a reliable conclusion. If this is the case for you, be sure to ask your agent if they know this attorney, call other local brokerages to see if they have any insight, or ask the attorney for references from previous clients.

Insurance Agent/Broker

One of the biggest concerns many investors have when buying property where a tenant will be involved is the liability they're opening themselves up to. This leads to a common question—to LLC or not to LLC? Should a property be purchased in a business entity, such as an LLC, to help shield the investor from liability, given the protections usually provided by an LLC? That is the most common solution investors look toward for liability protection, but it's not the only one. Another way to protect yourself as an investor, outside of forming a business entity, is to get a comprehensive insurance policy.

ALERT

There is a common misconception among new real estate investors that investment properties must be purchased using a business entity, such as an LLC. While this is effective for protection in theory, it is difficult to implement in practice when purchasing small multifamily or single-family properties because most lenders will not lend to business entities on these property types using the loan products you're looking for.

Similar to the legal documents used during closing, the details of an insurance policy can be difficult to understand. That's exactly why you use professionals that do this for a living every day. Just as you hire an attorney to review your legal documents, you should work with an insurance agent or broker to help you find a policy that fits your needs and to make sure you understand it inside and out.

If your agent works with a lot of investors, which they probably do since you picked them as the first member of your team, ask them for a referral to an insurance agent that their previous investor clients have used in the past. As with all the professionals on your team, you want an insurance agent who is experienced with real estate specifically and ideally has worked with investors. That way they already understand your needs as an investor and the important nuances of owning a rental property in your area. If your real estate agent does not have any recommended insurance agents, you can call other brokerages in the area and ask for their recommendations. You can also check online review platforms to help you build a list of potential insurance agents to work with that you can vet further before making a decision.

Property Manager

Should you self-manage or hire out management to a third-party property manager? Many investors face this dilemma when they're purchasing rental properties, which can include house hacks if a multiunit property is being purchased. It can also come into play for house hackers once they have decided to leave the property they had been house hacking.

For now, let's assume you are going to hire a third-party property manager. In Chapter 11, you'll learn about the different options and you can choose which is actually best for you.

> **FACT**
>
> The term "property manager" is often used to refer to a property management company, rather than an individual manager, but in the real estate world, it refers to the individual.

The property management team member was strategically placed at this point in the list because you will generally need the five professionals discussed previously first. And if you do decide to get a property manager, you may not need all the professionals discussed after this. An experienced property manager will have an in-house team of handymen, electricians, plumbers, carpenters, and so on, or they'll have built strong relationships with quality professionals that you can use to manage your rental unit(s). Therefore, if you do decide to use a third-party property manager, they will have all of this covered, and you won't have to build the relationships yourself.

Having a property manager can help you avoid a lot of the work you would otherwise have to do as a landlord, making your rentals almost entirely passive. You will still have some work to do, known as "managing the manager," but assuming your property manager is experienced, there should be little oversight and time required on your part—which provides you with a truly passive income. An inept property manager, however, can end up costing you a lot of money, time, and headaches, in various ways, from accepting the inappropriate tenants, not fixing repairs as they arise, failing to use high-quality and reasonably priced construction professionals, having poor financial reporting, and so on.

How do you find the best property managers? Similar to the other real estate professionals you have already found, you'll want to use your real estate agent when possible, refer to online review platforms, and conduct interviews yourself. Your agent probably knows property managers that their investor clients have used successfully in the past—this is usually the best place to start. If they do not have any recommendations, your agent should at least have some idea about property management companies in the area and their reputation. You can also build a list of potential property managers by looking online for highly rated property management companies or searching on Google for "property managers + [your investment city]." Once you have your list, whether it comes from your real estate agent's recommendations or online sources, conduct a thorough interview process with them to ensure that they offer all the services you require, their fee is reasonable, and they're experienced.

Following is a list of questions you can ask your potential property manager to help determine if they are a good fit for you:

- What services do you offer?

- How many rental units do you currently manage? Are you focused on a specific niche (short-term rentals, traditional rentals, house hack units, and so on)?
- What is the highest number of rental units you managed at one time?
- Do you specialize in one property type (i.e., single family, small multifamily, apartment buildings, and so on)?
- How do you determine the current market rent?
- Does your company's leadership team invest in rental properties in this area?
- What are the time requirements of our contract? Am I able to cancel at any time?
- What are your management fees? What are your additional fees on top of your base fee?
- What fees do you charge if/when a property is vacant?
- If I decide I want to sell my property, am I required to list it with you?
- Do you offer electronic deposits (i.e., direct deposit) for your clients?
- What is your process for collecting rent from tenants?
- Are you willing to only accept tenants that meet my predetermined criteria? If not, do you have an eviction warranty or screening guarantee?
- How do you market vacant units/properties?
- What is your average vacancy time?
- Do you mark up maintenance and repairs?
- What does your financial reporting package consist of? What is its frequency?

Handyman, Electrician, Plumber, HVAC, Carpenter

You may or may not need to find these five professionals yourself, depending on if you self-manage or hire out to a third-party property manager. If you are going to hire your property management out, you can skip to the Virtual Assistant section. If you are self-managing and need to find and manage these professionals yourself, read on.

No one wants to overpay for repairs on a property, whether it's for an investment or their primary residence, but it seems investors are even more critical of this, as it impacts their investment returns. When it's your primary residence, if your shower breaks, you just want it fixed as fast as possible so you and your family can get back to being clean. With a rental unit, investors are generally more concerned with preserving their capital and increasing their returns by being conscious of repair costs. As an investor, you need high-quality, reliable professionals to complete the repairs on your properties, but you also want their prices to be reasonable—which usually means less than what they'd charge a typical homeowner. If you're just beginning your investing journey, or you don't have a lot of units in a specific area, you probably have little negotiating power. However, if you own multiple units and plan to scale in that area, you can negotiate with the professional to offer you a discounted rate on their work, with the understanding that you're building a long-term relationship and that they'll receive additional work from you in the future for the rest of your portfolio. It doesn't help investors that, as of this writing, fewer people than ever are going into trades (plumbing, HVAC, electrical, and so on), meaning there are fewer experienced tradespeople to work with, leading to lower supply and higher demand—which ultimately erodes some of your negotiating power.

In most cases, your real estate agent should have relationships with reasonably priced, experienced professionals that they can refer you to. If not, the two best ways to find these professionals are through your real estate agent and using a contractor-specific search engine, such as Angi (formerly Angie's List) or HomeAdvisor. Professionals on these platforms generally aren't the most affordable, but if they're highly rated, which you can verify online, they're often a good option. Once you have worked with them, you can tell them your plan and how you'd like to build a long-term relationship with them in which they will be your go-to person for their trade work. At this point, you can negotiate a better rate than the initial quote you received.

Of course, you can also conduct a simple Google search and look for highly rated contractors in your area. This is just one of the many ways that technology is revolutionizing how real estate investing works.

As with all professionals, be sure to do your due diligence and have a conversation with the professional before you hire them. Their high ratings are a good indicator of that level of service continuing for you, but there are no guarantees. Give them a call, ask questions, get references, and make sure you feel comfortable with them based on the information you've learned.

Landscaper/Landscaping Company

You might be thinking, "Is a landscaping company really that important for my team?" Maybe they're not as important as your real estate agent or property manager, but landscapers provide a service that is often overlooked. If you were to buy a single-family property purely as a rental, you can and probably should write into your lease that the tenant is required to maintain the landscaping around the house. In this case, you probably would not need a landscaper for that property. However, if you own a multifamily property or are house hacking, it becomes more difficult to write this requirement into the lease.

> **FACT**
>
> One way around this is to offer a rent discount to a tenant that would be willing to be responsible for the landscaping—that can be a great way to solve this problem.

Assuming none of the previous options work and you do need to have a third party handle the landscaping at your property, or you choose to go that route solely because you don't want to do it yourself, it is good to have this in place before it is needed. When you're new to real estate, you probably won't give much thought to landscaping. With so many other things going on and the stress of buying your house hack, there's a good chance you will overlook landscaping. Thankfully, it isn't as important as some of the other major professionals you need on your team, but you do not want to be left scrambling when the issue comes about.

As with all real estate professionals, start by asking your real estate agent. If they know someone, you can probably just use their contact, assuming you're comfortable with them. If your real estate agent doesn't have any connections, you can simply follow similar steps from the previous sections—look for a highly rated, reasonably priced professional on search engines like Google, Angi, or HomeAdvisor or a review site like Yelp, and give them a call. You should not have to spend a significant amount of time hiring this team member. If you find someone that has great reviews, comes well recommended, has reasonable prices, and you enjoyed your initial conversation with them, you can confidently move forward without much worry.

Locksmith

Ah, the locksmith—an often-overlooked professional that can be valuable on your investing journey. This may not be the first person you'll think of when buying investment properties, but you'll be thankful that you were prepared if/when you need them, especially if you're self-managing.

Most leases include a provision that tenants are responsible for the issues that arise from being locked out of a home or other similar situations where a locksmith may be needed. However, if it is not considered up front, and therefore left out of the lease, you will be left rushing around to find a locksmith immediately available to help. Not only that, but if you had considered this up front, you could have made your tenant's life easier by having a locksmith recommendation ready to give them, rather than leaving them to figure it out on their own.

It's also beneficial to have a locksmith on your team to help with changing locks as soon as you close on the property. You don't necessarily need a locksmith for this; you could use a handyman or maybe even your agent if they're handy. If you search online, there are many horror stories from investors who didn't change the locks on their new property right away. You don't know how many people have keys to that property—the previous owner could've given one to everyone they know and never changed the locks. This isn't mentioned to scare you—most of the time, it's not an issue—rather, it is mentioned to help you be prepared and bring light to a situation you may not have considered before.

The process for finding a locksmith is nearly identical to the process for a landscaper/landscaping company; you can repeat the steps from that section. Put simply, ask your real estate agent first, and if that fails, use online platforms to find a reasonably priced, highly rated professional.

Virtual Assistant

You can buy a house hack, even multiple house hacks, successfully without a virtual assistant, but the question is, should you? If you've hired a third-party property manager, you probably won't need a virtual assistant—at least for a while. However, if you are self-managing, a virtual assistant can be very helpful. Once you've figured out your processes and have your list of team members assembled, hiring a virtual assistant can be a smart next step.

If you put effective processes into place, your virtual assistant should be able to step in and take over everything on your plate and make your business almost entirely passive. You may need to review their work until you fully trust them and understand their quality of work, or you may need to assist if a major issue comes up, but for the most part, they can make your real estate business significantly more passive for you.

ALERT

If you are working *in* your real estate business rather than *on* your real estate business, you have effectively purchased yourself another job. This is rarely the goal for real estate investors—most are after the passive income. Virtual assistants allow you to stop performing tasks like an employee with a job and instead have you acting as an owner of a business.

When it comes to finding and hiring a virtual assistant, there are many different ways you can find a freelancer to fill this role—new platforms are popping up frequently. You don't even have to find someone online—you could find someone local, or you could even choose to work with a family member.

However, one of the most proven ways to find this individual is through Upwork. The site is easy to use, it has a great pool of candidates, it allows you to track the freelancer's screen to ensure they are doing the work they were assigned, it's affordable, and it's quick to set up.

One of the great things about Upwork is that there are a ton of freelancers on the platform. One of the downsides of Upwork is that there are a ton of freelancers on the platform. It's good and bad—it's great there are a lot of people to choose from, but it can be overwhelming or difficult to choose just one.

> **ESSENTIAL**
>
> If you're interested in learning more about hiring virtual assistants and freelancers, Chris Ducker's book *Virtual Freedom: How to Work with Virtual Staff to Buy More Time, Become More Productive, and Build Your Dream Business* is a worthwhile resource to consider.

What's great about nearly everything you've learned in this chapter, as well as what you'll learn throughout the rest of this book, is that you can apply it to other types of real estate investing too. If you finish this book and you decide that house hacking isn't for you, or maybe you just want to start with a different strategy first, your valuable time hasn't been wasted by reading this book because you can apply all of these strategies and principles to your investing, whether you choose house hacking or traditional rental properties.

CHAPTER 6

Finding the Right Property for Your House Hack

Think about this: How can you find a deal if you don't know exactly *what* you want to find and *where* you want to find it? Even if a good deal presented itself, how would you know? You may have missed a good deal in the past because you didn't know what or where you were looking. In order to not miss any more good deals going forward, you must first define *what* it is you're looking for. In this chapter, you'll learn exactly how to define what type of property you're looking for and how to find it.

Property Type

New investors often say they can't find any good deals. Ask yourself this: What are you looking for and where are you looking for it? If you can't answer that question specifically, how do you know you can't find any good deals? If this is you, you are not alone. It is a very common mistake a lot of new real estate investors make.

It is important to start with the "what" before you move on to the "where." You may have thought you found a great market to buy your house hack in, only to realize after spending time finding that market that the types of properties you are looking for are not available in that market, or the inventory is too low, maybe even nonexistent. If you are specifically looking for a side-by-side, townhouse-style duplex, but the market you have found does not have any of those properties in the town, or there are not any for sale, it might not be the right market for you.

You do need to be very specific with what you are looking to purchase. It is not enough to simply say that you are looking for a duplex or a triplex. There are a lot of nuances that can go into those two property types. Do you want a townhouse-style duplex and a garden- or apartment-style triplex? Maybe vice versa? Be sure to define exactly which property type and floor plan you would like in your property.

ESSENTIAL

If you really liked a specific market and wanted to get creative, you could certainly try to find off-market deals. If the property type you are looking for exists in the given market, but there just aren't any for sale, you may have luck going directly to the current owners and buying off-market.

It is also important to define exactly what it is you want to buy so you have a better chance of not drifting away from your true desires. If you spent time looking for multiple markets to house hack in, only to realize you couldn't find the type of property you were looking for, you might eventually start to sacrifice your nonnegotiables just to get a deal. As your requirements drift, you might try to convince yourself a property is acceptable or a good deal. House hacking inherently requires sacrifice. You may need to drift slightly from your initial requirements and compromise, but be aware that this is a slippery slope and can lead to a negative house hacking experience, both financially and mentally, if you allow yourself to drift too far.

ALERT

Create an investing journal to ensure you stick to your nonnegotiables and do not drift too far. In your journal, you should write the date, type of property you are looking for, and a few bullet points as to why that property is what you want. It may be obvious and fresh in your mind now, but in the future, it may not be, and you want to be able to reference this later.

Defining exactly what it is that you are looking for does not mean that it can only be one property type. You do not want to define, say, five or six property types, but choosing one or two is acceptable. As an example, you may be open to duplexes and triplexes, or maybe even one-to-four-unit properties, but no single family.

If you do define more than one property type, be sure to not sacrifice the details of your definition due to the increased quantity. You must still define if you want garden-style or townhouse-style, if you want the units side-by-side or if you want them up-and-down. What kind of parking arrangement do you want? Is a shared driveway okay, or must parking all be separate?

It is easier to be detailed when you choose only one property type, so if you choose more than one, be sure to not sacrifice your details just to save time or effort.

Property Condition

Knowing which type of property you're looking for is a great start, but you must also know the condition in which you would be willing to accept these properties. For example, if you have decided that you are open to duplexes, but you have not defined the condition you are looking for, it is almost as if you did not decide on the property type at all. You may find a duplex that is turnkey, or rent-ready, but this may not align with your goals if you are looking for a property with a bit more opportunity for forced equity (see sidebar). Likewise, a duplex in need of rehab may not align with your goals if you are looking for a turnkey property that requires minimal work to get started.

FACT

Equity in real estate is the difference between what a property is worth and what is owed on that property. Forced equity, sometimes referred to as "forced appreciation," is when you make improvements to a property that cost less than you gain in value for those improvements. By intentionally making those improvements to drive up the value of the property, you are "forcing" equity.

You may need to prioritize major repairs, since they can take considerable capital and time to handle. However, depending on your situation, your definition of what is acceptable for your property condition may need to be even more detailed. For example, you may be reluctant to house hack but agree to under certain conditions; for example, if the property is in pristine condition and has certain features. It is important to understand and define all the criteria you need in a property, even the most minute details, before beginning your search.

These details may include items such as the paint color and condition, the condition of decks and patios, whether or not significant landscaping is necessary to achieve your satisfaction, and the list goes on. There are many items to consider. Make a list of those items that are most important to you to ensure you have clear criteria for type and condition.

Tenant Desirability

Everything you have thought about and written in your investing journal so far represents *your* criteria. However, you are not the only one to consider in this equation when defining your property type and condition. If you are planning to house hack, that means you will have tenants. That may mean roommates in a single-family home or in a separate unit, depending on which type of property you choose. You must also consider the type of tenants your property will draw interest from and how your decisions may impact your potential tenants' desires, which in turn will impact the demand for your rental unit.

> **FACT**
>
> Supply and demand is an economic theory that has a significant impact on real estate, both when selling or purchasing a property as well as renting a unit. This theory states that the lower the supply and the higher the demand drives prices higher, and vice versa.

If you own a traditional rental property, your goal is likely to have reliable and polite tenants; otherwise, you have more headaches and make less money. But if you did end up with noisy or inconsiderate tenants in a traditional rental property, your personal living situation likely would not be negatively impacted. Unfortunately, undesirable tenants in a house hack situation would probably negatively impact your personal living situation because they live in a unit connected to where you live, or even in the same home if this is a rent-by-the-room situation.

Because your personal living situation is more impacted by house hack tenants than in other real estate investing situations, such as traditional rentals, it is important to consider what type of tenants the property you are looking for will draw interest from. If you purchase a single-family house and use a rent-by-the-room strategy, that is going to draw interest from a different type of tenant than, say, a large three- or four-bedroom townhouse-style unit in a duplex. Neither of these situations is necessarily better than the other; it just depends on what type of tenant you are hoping to attract.

In the case of a single-family house that is being rented by the room, you are probably not going to attract families or older tenants. These property types usually draw the most interest from young people and/or single, working professionals. If you are an older individual with a family and kids, this may not be the right type of tenant for you. However, if you are a recent college graduate who is just starting their career, this type of tenant might be perfect for you!

If you are hacking a duplex, triplex, or fourplex, the type of tenants you attract is going to depend on the specific characteristics of the property. In the case of one-bedroom units, potential interested tenants will probably be similar to those attracted to the single-family rent-by-the-room strategy mentioned previously. If the units have three or four bedrooms, you are more likely to get interest from families. In general, families tend to stay at a property longer and take better care of it, which can lead to fewer turnover costs and less stress. There are pros and cons to nearly all types of tenants—there is no one-size-fits-all solution. Consider what you are most comfortable managing and living next to.

If you were to go with a strategy from Chapter 4 that is a bit more out of the ordinary, such as short-term rentals or vacation properties, you will need to spend some time thinking about what types of people that strategy will draw interest from. The strategies outlined in Chapter 3, such as rent-by-the-room and multifamily properties, are more common and are employed by far more people. Neither type of strategy is better or worse, but each one provides more data points to learn from and allows you to get an idea for what you might experience if you went down a particular path. With an unconventional strategy, you will need to think for yourself and create your own ideas about which types of people will be interested in that rental offering.

In addition to the type of tenants that are interested in your property, the property type can also impact the amount of demand for your rental unit(s) overall. Nearly every location is going to be impacted differently by property types. It is best to research the area you are looking to purchase in to determine which property type is most in demand. You can also connect with local real estate agents and property managers to get their opinions as well.

Let's look at a few of the most popular situations and how your property type decision could impact the demand for your rental unit. If you are looking to buy a duplex in a location with a lot of single-family homes and/or a lot of new-build apartments, the demand for your rental unit may be a bit low. That does not mean you would not be able to find a high-quality tenant; it just means that you may have a more difficult time and/or would not be able to demand the market rent. If someone can rent a single-family home or a newly built apartment unit for the same cost as your duplex unit, what would attract them to rent your unit? If they have lived in this area for a significant period, they may have become accustomed to the most common living situations in that area, which yours is not.

On the other hand, if you purchase a duplex in a town that has hundreds of duplexes, renters in that area are likely more used to that type of living situation and would be more open to renting your unit. The same can be said for single-family houses, triplexes, and fourplexes. If the property type is more common in a given area, the more likely you are to have tenants that are willing and interested in that type of property, which increases the demand for your rental unit(s).

In addition to the property type, your potential tenants are going to care about the condition of the property. This will impact both how much you can charge for rent *and* the demand you receive for your unit(s). Single-family homes are often expected to be in better condition with better materials than an apartment-style unit in a fourplex. If you are going to buy a single-family to house hack in an area where there are a lot of other nice houses, your potential tenants will probably require a similar-quality property for themselves. If your property is in an area where there are not many nice single-family houses, you may be able to get away with a slightly lower-quality finish for your house hack, or you could potentially charge more in rent if your property is above average. The same is true for duplexes, triplexes, and fourplexes as well.

There are a few other dynamics at play with the type of property you choose. As you add more units, the expected quality within the property typically decreases. In other words, duplexes are typically expected to be nicer than triplexes, and triplexes are expected to be nicer than fourplexes. Also, most potential tenants expect townhouse-style units to be nicer than garden- or apartment-style units. Townhouse-style units are typically side-by-side, whereas garden- and apartment-style units are up-and-down, with the former being more desirable than the latter due to people's preference for living next to each other rather than on top of each other. A townhouse-style triplex may be nicer than a garden- or apartment-style duplex, despite duplexes often being considered to be nicer. Of course, these are not hard rules, and there are plenty of areas where this is not the case, but it is common in many markets.

Acceptable Financial Metrics

Not only does the property type impact the types of tenants you will draw interest from; it will also impact the potential returns you can achieve. If you remember from Chapter 1, there is a relationship between the amount of comfort you give up and a property's profitability when it comes to house hacking. In a single-family house, you give up the most comfort, but you probably will receive some of the highest profits. Similarly, in a fourplex, you give up the most comfort but receive some of the highest gains. In a duplex, you give up the least comfort but sacrifice some of your potential profits.

In Chapter 1, you were asked to consider whether you were looking to purchase a house hack in order to live for free, live at a reduced rate, or make a profit each month. Now, you need to answer this question using actual numbers that are acceptable for you and also consider how each property type and floor plan could impact those numbers.

If your goal is to live for free, that is self-explanatory and not much analysis is needed past that. Your acceptable financial metric is for your rental income to equal your total mortgage cost. However, if you want to reduce your housing costs or make a profit, you need to clarify what those numbers mean. How much of your mortgage are you willing to cover yourself, after rental income? Is there an acceptable range or is there just a maximum threshold you do not want to cross? Is $500 per month the most you are willing to pay toward the mortgage? $250? $1,000? When you are looking to earn a profit, what is an acceptable amount of profit for you? What do you consider to be worthwhile? Is there a minimum that you will accept, and everything above that is a bonus?

FACT

You calculate your cost of living when house hacking by determining your total mortgage cost, including principal, interest, taxes, insurance, and PMI, then subtracting your total rental income. The difference between your rental income and total mortgage cost is your profit, if rental income is higher, or your living cost, if rental income is lower.

There are no right or wrong answers to these questions, but they are part of the criteria you must define before you start your property search. The criteria for your property search outlined in this chapter are all required. You cannot skip one piece, or the process will not work how it should. If you define your property type and condition but you do not define your acceptable financial metrics, what happens when you find the perfect property but the numbers do not make sense? Instead of living for free, as you wanted, you are instead paying $1,000 per month toward your mortgage. What if you find a property in the condition you like and the numbers are amazing, but the property type does not match your desires and you are unhappy living there? The important part of defining your criteria is not *what* you choose; rather, it is *that* you choose.

How to Find the Property

At this point, you have taken the time to define exactly what it is you are looking to buy for your house hack. You know exactly which type of property it is, which floor plan you want, the condition of it, and what your acceptable financial metrics are. Now, how do you *actually* find that property?

Decades ago, finding properties to purchase was significantly harder and more time-consuming than it is today. Not only that, but there were high barriers to entry. To see what was for sale, you needed access to the multiple listing service, also known as the MLS. To access the MLS, you needed to be a licensed real estate agent or broker, which means paying a fee and passing the test(s). As a typical individual looking to purchase a property, you do not have access to this information. You need to go to an agent or broker and have them send you the information you want. As the buyer, you would tell the agent exactly what you are looking for, then they would look in the MLS or contact other real estate professionals in their network to see if there were any properties available that matched your criteria.

Today, the process is much simpler, faster, and more efficient, but there are some drawbacks. Decades ago, the real estate market was not as efficient as it is today. Due to this inefficiency, it was often easier to purchase a property. There were not hundreds or thousands of people searching the Internet every day in the exact area you are looking to buy in, which meant less competition for you as a buyer. You did not have a lot of competing offers on properties you were interested in. Technology has made access to property listings significantly easier, which is great when searching for a property, but it has also increased competition and made it more difficult to get your offer accepted. The information is no longer accessible to only a relatively small group of people—hundreds of thousands of people have access to all the same information with a few clicks on their smartphones.

The simplest way to find the property you are looking for is to use a third-party service, such as Zillow, on your smartphone or computer. Simply enter the location you are looking to buy in. Most third-party sites give you the option to enter specific criteria for the property you are searching for. Enter the criteria that you have already defined. Hit "Search," and that's it—you should see a list of appropriate properties pop up on your screen.

Not all of the criteria you have defined so far will be among the options you can select on these third-party sites. For example, you probably won't be able to choose which type of condition you would like the property to be in. There are some shortcuts, such as not including foreclosed properties in your search if you are looking for a move-in, rent-ready property, since foreclosures typically are not in the best condition. You can narrow down the available properties as much as possible using the criteria on the platform, then removing potential properties that do not fit your other criteria by going through the listing's images. In many cases, if the platform does not provide an option for all of your criteria, you can determine the rest by going through photos or looking at the property's description in the listing.

These online platforms are replacing what real estate agents used to do for their customers before technology allowed for these types of sites. Instead of the agent searching through the MLS to look for properties their buyer might be interested in, these online platforms access the MLS directly and provide that information to their users. Real estate agents still provide significant value in a real estate transaction, but online real estate platforms have mostly eliminated the need for real estate agents in the searching process. Now, once you have found a property you are interested in, you contact your real estate agent and ask them to schedule a showing for you.

In addition to websites that are real estate–specific, such as Zillow, there are other online platforms you can use to find a property to purchase. Typically, real estate–specific platforms are your best option, but plenty of people have had success on sites that are not focused solely on real estate, like Facebook Marketplace and Craigslist. Properties listed on these and similar sites that do not pull from the MLS data are typically for sale by owner, which means they are not being sold with a real estate agent and probably are not listed on the MLS.

Some people try to sell their properties themselves without using a real estate agent. There are many reasons why a property seller might believe this is the best route, but the most common reason is to avoid paying the commission to a real estate agent. With a $300,000 property and a 4 percent commission, a seller could potentially save themselves $12,000 by selling the property themselves. There are reasons why this may not be a good idea, but some sellers only look at the financial piece of it and do not consider the value real estate agents provide in exchange for that commission.

FACT

According to Redfin's research, the average real estate commission paid by sellers in the United States is between 5 and 6 percent. However, real estate agents' commissions are typically not fixed and can be negotiated with their broker.

From the buyer's perspective, there is nothing wrong with buying from a for-sale-by-owner and/or someone who is not using a real estate agent. However, it is important to consider how, as a buyer, that is going to impact your relationship with your real estate agent. If you think back to earlier in this book, you learned that real estate agents are usually "free" for buyers. That does not mean, however, that they do not make any money from the transaction. Very few things are truly free, and real estate agents certainly do not work for nothing. Typically, the seller's agent splits the transaction's total commission with the buyer's agent. Using the 4 percent commission example, a common situation would be for the seller's agent to keep 2 percent, or half of the total commission, and give the buyer's agent the other 2 percent. Since the buyer's agent is getting paid from the seller's agent, the buyer's agent does not collect any money from the buyer. In a for-sale-by-owner transaction, since there is no seller's agent, there is no commission to be split with the buyer's agent. This means that the buyer's agent may not want to assist with that transaction or that they will still want to earn their normal commission, which would have to be paid by the buyer.

One of the beneficial aspects of real estate investing is that there are nearly an unlimited number of different ways to find a deal. There are books written about the next few strategies that will be briefly discussed here. These strategies are all common in the overall real estate world, but not the most common when house hacking. Each strategy will be covered in detail, but they are absolutely viable for house hacking. If you are willing to get creative, put in the time and effort, you can use these strategies to find your house hack. These strategies include getting leads from friends and/or family, wholesaling, driving for dollars, direct-mail marketing, search engine optimization, social media, and pay-per-click advertising.

Friends and Family

Your friends and family have their own friends and family, and their friends and family have their own friends and family. It goes on and on, covering a lot of people. There is a chance that one of those people is selling their property, thinking about selling their property, or knows someone who is selling. By telling as many of your friends and family as possible, the word may eventually reach someone who has a property that is a good fit for you. It can be a bit daunting to share with the world what you are working on, especially if it is new to you, but your existing network can't help you if you keep it a secret.

Wholesaling

Before you can purchase a property from a wholesaler, it is important to understand how the strategy works. The general strategy of wholesaling in real estate is very similar to wholesaling in other industries. Many people are probably familiar with how this model works outside of real estate, but did not realize it existed within real estate. In other industries, items are purchased at a discount because they are bought in large quantities. Then, the buyer resells those same goods at a higher price. The original seller is willing to reduce the amount they could sell the goods for because it takes less work for them to sell in bulk, whereas the secondhand seller, the wholesaler, is willing to do a bit more work and sell in smaller quantities to earn a profit by buying goods in bulk.

In real estate, a wholesaler will get a property under contract, meaning they have an agreement to purchase the property for less than they think it is worth, then they assign that contract to a different buyer for a higher amount and collect the difference as their profit for their work in finding the deal. Let's look at an example with real numbers.

A wholesaler learns that a local property owner just passed away and their children, who live out of state, are going to be inheriting the property. Like many out-of-state people who acquire a property from an inheritance, this seller did not want to put in the time and money to sell the property for the highest possible amount (i.e., market value). Because a wholesaler can get the property under contract for less than it is worth, the seller decides they would rather sell the property for less money to someone who is willing to do the work. The property has a market value of $250,000, but it needs quite a bit of repairs and to be listed on the MLS by a real estate agent in order to sell it for that price. Because of this, the wholesaler was able to acquire the property for $165,000. The wholesaler has no desire to do the work and resell the property. Instead, the wholesaler will take the contract for the property to a buyer who is willing to do the extra work to resell it to a different buyer for a profit. The buyers who typically purchase contracts, and therefore the underlying property, from wholesalers are real estate investors, specifically flippers. There are times when rental property investors will purchase from wholesalers, such as a house hacker, but the most common buyer is a flipper.

Since real estate investors who flip properties typically try to acquire properties at 70 percent of their after repair value (see sidebar), this flipper is willing to pay $175,000 for the property the wholesaler has under contract ($175,000 is 70 percent of $250,000). The wholesaler has the property under contract for $165,000 and has found a real estate flipper who is willing to pay $175,000 for the property. The difference of $10,000 is the wholesaler's profit on this deal. As a house hacker, you can purchase your property from the end seller—in this case, the real estate flipper—or you can purchase it from the wholesaler. Typically, flippers list their properties on the MLS with a real estate agent, so you may not even realize you are purchasing from a flipper. However, if you go directly to the wholesaler, you will know because there usually are no agents involved, similar to a for-sale-by-owner property. By going directly to the wholesaler, you may be able to get a better deal than you could by buying from the flipper.

Since many of the properties sold through wholesalers need significant rehabs, you must consider if this approach fits in with your property condition criteria defined earlier in this chapter. Also, buying a property that needs significant rehab can limit the types of loans you can use, which means you might not be able to take advantage of the beneficial loan terms and products offered to owner-occupants. Buying from a wholesaler can be a great way to get a property at a discount with built-in equity, but it may not be the right approach for someone just getting started in real estate.

Other Methods

With other ways of finding properties to purchase, such as driving for dollars, direct-mail marketing, search engine optimization, social media, and pay-per-click, you are moving up the acquisition chain in front of wholesalers. Wholesalers typically use these strategies to get properties under contract for a discount to the market value, then go through the process previously described. Instead of buying from the wholesaler, you can remove them from the equation and go directly to the seller by using one of these strategies.

> **ESSENTIAL**
>
> There is a chain of acquisitions with real estate properties. The closer you get to the beginning of the chain, the better deal you receive. The first spot on the chain is the property's seller, then wholesalers, then flippers, and, finally, the final property buyer.

- Driving for dollars involves driving around your area to look for properties that are showing signs of distress, which means they might be for sale.
- Direct-mail marketing involves writing to property owners (usually on a postcard) that you are interested in acquiring their property.
- Search engine optimization involves creating a website and using real estate–related keywords in your content that will bring up your site when people search for those terms.
- Pay-per-click ads involve purchasing online ads that tell viewers you are looking to acquire properties in their area. The goal of pay-per-click

ads is the same as for search engine optimization: for someone to come across your website or ads and contact you to sell their property.

- Using social media to spread the word is like telling your friends and family but on a broader scale. Create a post on social media that establishes your personal brand and lets people know what you want to purchase, and you could have thousands of people keeping their eyes and ears open for you. If any of them find a deal that fits your criteria, they will send it your way.

When it comes to house hacking, especially your first one, the best strategy is to purchase from the MLS through an online platform with a real estate agent. As you get more experience in real estate, you can probably implement one of the other acquisition strategies discussed in this chapter to get an even better deal.

CHAPTER 7

Finding the Right Market
for Your House Hack

Location. Location. Location. It's one of the most—
if not *the* most—important things in real estate.
How can you find great locations to buy a property
when you are looking to house hack? In this chapter,
you'll learn how by using data and leveraging other
people—specifically real estate professionals.

Using Demographic Data

Some investors have great success going off their gut feeling or intuition. However, that is hard to replicate and is not sustainable, whereas data can be used over and over to make reliable, fact-based decisions.

There are six key data points to help you establish if a city is a good place to invest. Each city has good neighborhoods and bad neighborhoods, but these six data points will enable you to determine if the city is worth investigating to find the good neighborhoods. That's where expert opinions can come in very handy.

Let's start the analysis at a high level by looking at the city as a whole, then we will dive into the specifics of how to find appropriate neighborhoods for you by using real estate experts. The six key data points used to analyze cities are population growth, income growth, property value growth, crime level, crime change, and job growth.

ESSENTIAL

The rate of population growth is calculated as the ending number minus the beginning number, divided by the beginning number, multiplied by one hundred. As an example, today's population level minus the year 2000's population level, divided by the year 2000's population level, multiplied by one hundred equals the population growth. You can find a video walk-through of calculating the population growth at https://everythinghousehacking.com/calculating-population-growth.

Population Growth

The population growth data point looks at how many more people currently live in an area than the year 2000. With a declining or stagnant population, it is unlikely that property values and incomes would increase, which leads to subpar rental property conditions. As a baseline, a growth rate of 20 percent or more is considered satisfactory by many investors' standards. Some investors are okay with less than 20 percent, and some may require more than 20 percent, but in general, 20 percent is a good rule. Also, regarding population, it is often wise to look at cities with a population of greater than fifty thousand because a population that is significantly less than that has a higher chance of not having enough rental demand or population growth. This is not a hard rule, nor is it a requirement in all scenarios, but it is a commonly used rule.

Income Growth

The income growth data point looks at how much a median household income has grown since the year 2000. With a declining or stagnant median household income, rents and property values are unlikely to increase. As a guideline, target cities where the median income has grown by more than 30 percent since the year 2000.

Property Value Growth

The property value growth data point looks at how much a median house or condo value has gone up since the year 2000. With declining or stagnant median property values, it is difficult to take advantage of one of the major pillars of real estate investing—appreciation. While you may not want to invest solely for appreciation, it can be an advantage when possible, as it can oftentimes generate wealth faster than cash flow alone. A recommended benchmark for property value growth is 40 percent since the year 2000.

Crime Level

The crime-level data point measures the current crime level in your chosen city as of the most recent year with available data. In areas with a high incidence of crime, people are more likely to move away, property values will fall, and income will not grow, all of which make for subpar real estate investing conditions. When utilizing City-Data.com and its crime index, a general benchmark for a city is a crime index of less than 500 (you can find all six benchmarks at https://everythinghousehacking.com/demographic-data-benchmarks).

Crime Change

Crime-change data looks at how much the crime level of your chosen city has increased or decreased since the year 2000. If crime is trending down, that could indicate that a city is improving and is a good opportunity for investing. If crime level is trending up, that could mean that the city's quality is deteriorating, and it could be a trap for long-term, buy-and-hold real estate investors. If a city on the fringe of the recommended crime level or even above it has a declining crime rate, there could be an opportunity to invest in an area that is potentially improving. As a guideline, it is recommended to target a city with a 0 percent or negative crime-growth rate. Anything above 0 percent indicates that the crime level has increased, according to City-Data.com's crime index.

Job Growth

The job-growth data point measures the annual growth of jobs in your chosen city over the previous twelve months. If job growth is slowing or trending down, the city or the companies located there might be going through economic trouble. This trouble eventually flows down to the investor's tenants, who might eventually lose their jobs and be unable to pay rent. Strong job growth, however, usually means that the city and companies are doing well and prospering. This often leads to more job opportunities, increased wages, and more people moving to the area, which can bring higher demand for rentals and increased rents.

Real Estate Data Sources and Tools

You may be thinking, "Okay, that all makes sense. I understand the value in this data and the data-driven approach, but how can I get that data?"

The two main sources for the city-level data points are City-Data.com and the Department of Numbers. Neither of these sources are tailored specifically for real estate investors, but they provide comprehensive data and are easy to access.

To start your research, go to City-Data.com and click on the state you're interested in. You can look for cities that meet your minimum population requirement, or click on a specific city. On the city's page, you can find the first five data points. To find job growth information, you will need to visit the Department of Numbers website, as City-Data.com does not offer this.

Go to the Department of Numbers website (www.deptofnumbers .com/employment/metros/) and find the city you are interested in. Once you have located the city you are interested in, you will want to locate the "1-Year CES Jobs Percent Change" data. At this point, you have collected all six demographic data points necessary to complete your analysis of your selected city.

Technology has completely changed how people become investors and buy real estate. The availability of online information is just one example of how the investing world has changed. Decades ago, this data was not available, or it would take a very long time to find. Today, you can access this data for thousands of cities in a matter of minutes. As you continue to progress through this book, you will learn multiple other ways that technology has changed how people can invest in real estate.

Evaluating Specific Neighborhoods

Now that you have found cities that are promising, the next step is to figure out which neighborhoods you will want to invest in within that city. The best ways to do this are by using both real estate professionals and technology.

If you needed brain surgery, you would want to go to an experienced brain surgeon, right? If you needed a new transmission, you would want a mechanic who deals with transmissions almost every day, right? Well, it is no different with real estate. You want to find experienced professionals to get the information you need. There are four key resources you can use to find the appropriate neighborhoods in the cities you have identified. They are real estate agents and brokers, property managers, other real estate investors, and the online real estate platform Realtor.com.

If you bought real estate before 2010, many of these options were not available or were not at a large enough scale to really act as a great resource to investors. You may be thinking, "Real estate agents have been around since real estate started," and you'd be right. But what was *not* available was a way to easily connect with agents that were not local, nor was there a way to quickly gauge their level of experience. Thanks to online platforms, it is easy to find highly rated real estate agents and brokers in nearly any market, in just a few minutes. With a few clicks of a button, you have access to hundreds of agents in the area you are looking to purchase in, with reviews from past clients and the agent's contact information.

The agents and brokers in the area you are looking to purchase in have probably been buying and/or selling real estate in that area for years. They have helped many people before you buy property in that area, and they know all the intricacies and details that go into the process. Therefore, they typically have the expertise and information that can help you find the best areas to buy in and the places you may want to avoid.

If it is your first time purchasing in a new area and/or your first time working with a new agent, you should probably not rely on just one person to make a buying decision. You should verify the information you are given with other professionals. It is not necessarily an issue of trust, but sometimes they might have a different opinion of what is a "good" or "bad" area than you do. Everyone has a different paradigm in which they are viewing the world.

It is free to call and speak with real estate agents and brokers—take advantage of this. Call an agent and tell them your situation. Explain to them what you want to do. Then ask their opinion on the best and worst neighborhoods in which to invest in the city you have chosen. Not only do they know the area well; they also probably enjoy giving their opinion. People usually like to feel that their opinion is valued. Take notes on the information they give you. You can do this in a notebook, in a Word document, or even on a map. It can be helpful to print a physical copy of a map of the specific city to jot down notes and circle the relevant areas.

ALERT

Even though it is free to call real estate professionals, it is important to remember that their time is valuable and to be respectful of that. Real estate investing is entirely a relationship endeavor, and you do not want to start out on the wrong foot by taking advantage of someone's time.

Once you have taken notes from your conversation with the first agent, repeat the process with at least two more agents who work at different brokerages. Gathering opinions from three to five agents is generally a good rule when trying to learn about a new area. You can certainly do more, but it is not recommended to do any fewer than three. If the first three agents you speak with tell you almost the exact same information, then you probably have reliable data and can move forward, but if they vary wildly in their opinions, you will need to gather more information to make a sound decision. You may even need to speak with more than five agents until you feel comfortable with the information you are receiving.

Here are a few questions you can ask real estate agents to help determine which neighborhoods are a good fit for you:

- Which neighborhoods do you think are the nicest and safest?
- Why do you think that? How are other neighborhoods of less quality?

- Are you investing in real estate here? If so, which area(s) of the city are you investing in?
- What is the typical rent in those areas for [insert your specific property type(s) here]? How does that compare to other areas in the city?
- In which part of the city do you receive the highest rent for [insert your specific property type(s) here]?
- Where do you currently see a lot of other investors buying?
- Which parts of the city are people moving to? Why?
- Are there any major developments in the city that you are aware of that may positively or negatively impact a given area?

Property Managers

To further diversify the opinions you are receiving, you can also contact property managers. Real estate agents are great at giving advice on specific areas, but many agents only work with traditional home buyers and sellers, not investors.

> **ESSENTIAL**
>
> Property managers work specifically with rental property investors on a daily basis and therefore might have a better understanding of the current rental market than agents do. Many property managers are in charge of hundreds of units for various investors and most likely have a great pool of experience to draw from.

The same process you underwent for real estate agents can be replicated for property managers. You can also mix and match by getting opinions from both. Take notes on the information you learn and do not rely on just one or two property managers' opinions. Reach out to at least three to five different property managers, ideally from different companies.

Here are a few questions you can ask property managers to help determine which neighborhoods are a good fit for you:

- Are there any areas in [insert your city here] that you will not manage properties in? If so, why?
- Where do you see a lot of other investors acquiring properties right now?
- Which areas have you found are experiencing the lowest vacancy rates? What is the average vacancy rate for the worst, best, and average areas in the city?
- Which neighborhoods have seen steady and, ideally, growing rents?
- Of all the neighborhoods your current clients are investing in, where are they having the most success? Where are they experiencing the most issues?

Other Investors

Another source of information on neighborhoods is other real estate investors. One of the major issues with this approach is that there are a limited number of properties in the "good" neighborhoods, and other investors may not want to tell you exactly where they are. A lot of investors have an abundance mindset, meaning they know there are enough deals to go around, but you will come across some who are not willing to share information in an attempt to protect their favorite areas. This should not deter you from talking with other investors; just keep it in mind.

FACT

An abundance mindset is the idea and mentality that there is enough opportunity in the world for everyone to earn their share. The opposite is a scarcity mindset, where you believe that opportunities are always a zero-sum game—someone must lose in order for you to win.

Another way to get information from investors is to ask them where they are investing and which class of properties and neighborhoods they like to buy in from the standpoint of someone who is just curious, rather than as a potential competitor. However, just because someone is investing in a particular area does not mean that it is right for you, nor does it mean that you should blindly invest there. The other investor could have higher risk tolerance, they could be following a different strategy, or they could just run their real estate investing business differently than you want to. If that investor's property and neighborhood classes do match what you are targeting, you can use the information to determine which areas you might be willing to invest in. Speaking with other investors can certainly provide great insight; they are the ones doing the investing after all, but you need to ensure their advice aligns with what other real estate professionals—real estate agents and property managers—have told you. If it is wildly different, you may need to question the investor's motive and dig deeper.

Why You Shouldn't Follow the Crowd

Wouldn't it be much simpler to just follow the crowd and invest in the most popular cities that other investors are buying in? Not quite.

Investor interest can indicate that a market is worth investing in. However, there are three major reasons why you may not want to follow the crowd into a market. First, doing so does not reduce the research and analysis time or effort. Second, there is far more competition. Third, the demographic data for the six data points you just learned about may not be right for you.

Just because other investors are acquiring properties in a particular area, that does not mean every neighborhood in those cities is worthy of an investment, or a place you want to live. If you were to follow other investors into a city, you still have to do all the work to find the right neighborhoods. In reality, finding appropriate cities overall is relatively easy, thanks to online tools like City-Data.com and Department of Numbers, but finding the right neighborhoods still takes time. Therefore, you are not really saving much time or effort by following other investors into a city.

In popular markets, there is also significantly more competition. There are more people fighting for the same number of deals, and often the investors you are competing against are better capitalized than you, can close quicker, and have better relationships. These investors have already built all the right relationships and are the first to receive notification of any off-market deals or pocket listings from real estate agents and brokers. This takes the cream of the crop, and leaves you with the lower-quality deals. The increased competition leads to higher risk and lower returns.

The final reason for not following other investors is that these popular cities may not meet your criteria for the six key data points. Maybe you care more about population growth and crime level than you do property value growth. That opens an entirely new world of potential cities for you to purchase in that may be different from popular investor cities.

Accepting Your Current Location

Even if you use the strategies described in this chapter to find the perfect city and neighborhood to house hack in, it does not matter if you can't actually move there. There are many life circumstances that could keep you in the area you are residing in. Thankfully, there are still ways to use these strategies to make the best of your current location.

The chances are high that you could move twenty to sixty minutes away from where you currently live with relatively minor changes to your life. If you live in an area that is not ideal to house hack, but there is a great area within a sixty-minute drive, you could move there. It may take some sacrifice, which house hacking sometimes requires, but it is possible. Maybe you do not stay in your exact current location, but you remain in the same general location, within a certain proximity, which can be identified by using the strategies outlined in this chapter.

> **ESSENTIAL**
>
> Growth is rarely easy. Achieving your goals is almost never done without sacrifice. You do not have to move far from where you live to be a successful investor, but if you live in an area where house hacking isn't optimal, you must consider which you want more: comfort or achieving your goals.

If you must remain *exactly* where you are today, you can derive at least some peace from understanding the circumstances of where you live. Ignorance is not bliss. Not knowing the key demographic data points for where you live does not make the location any better. You can and should still go through the processes outlined in this chapter so you fully understand the area you live in. Doing so can help you make the best of your situation for however long you are there, or it can motivate you to try to find a way to move somewhere with better demographic data points. It may also enable you to make a less substantial move while still greatly improving the areas addressed by the data points.

You may not be able to move twenty to sixty minutes away. But what if you could move just a few blocks from where you live now and find a much better area? You may be able to find this out just by living there, but if you can't, then the data can help you find these opportunities.

CHAPTER 8

Analyzing House Hack Deals

In previous chapters, you learned that you can't find a property to buy if you do not know what you are looking for or where to look. The next step is to determine whether or not the property you found makes sense financially. It may be the perfect property in a great area, but the financials could be a deal breaker. In this chapter, you'll learn how to analyze each part of a house hack deal, such as the income, expenses, profitability, and the all-important post–house hack analysis.

Income Analysis

In its most simple form, a general income statement—for any business, not just real estate—starts with revenue or income at the top, then lists expenses, and has profit at the bottom. This is the same approach for analyzing a house hack deal. You start with income, then move on to expenses, and end with income. Think of it as an upside-down pyramid that is split into three sections horizontally. The section at the top is the largest, the middle section is the second-largest, and the bottom section, the tip of the pyramid, is the smallest. The top section represents your income, the middle section represents your expenses, and the bottom section represents your profit.

In a house hack deal, the most common type of revenue is your rental income. Regardless of which strategy you choose, conventional or unconventional, traditional or short-term, entire units or rent-by-the-room, or a strategy in between—your main income source is rental income. In Chapter 4, you learned how to find and estimate the rental income if you're using a short-term rental strategy. In this chapter, you will learn how to use that data in your deal analysis and how to estimate the rental income for traditional-rental house hacking strategies.

FACT

Not only does house hacking allow you to learn how to buy rental properties with training wheels; it also reduces the risk you have. When you buy a rental property, you typically have to put down 20–25 percent of the purchase as a down payment, which means you have more cash at stake to potentially lose if the deal goes wrong. With a house hack, you have less cash to lose if it goes wrong because you have a smaller down payment.

One of the benefits of house hacking is that it helps prepare you to become a real estate investor outside of house hacking properties. It teaches you how to make other types of real estate investments, similar to how training wheels help you learn how to ride a bike. You will be able to take the skills you learn in this book—like estimating rent and expenses and analyzing deals—and apply them to other real estate investing strategies you pursue in the future. Some of the material is house hacking–specific, but much of it is not. Much of it applies to other strategies as well.

For example, when you house hack a duplex and rent out the second unit you are not living in, that is essentially the same as a traditional rental unit. You would find and estimate the rent for that unit the same way you would if you had bought the duplex purely as a traditional rental, without living in one of the units. For a duplex as a traditional rental, you would just duplicate the process you went through for the one unit while house hacking for the second unit. If you were to use a short-term rental strategy while house hacking, you would follow the same process for finding and estimating rents if and when you purchase a traditional short-term rental investment property.

There is both an active, do-it-yourself approach and a passive, professional-based approach to estimating the rent for the rental units in your house hack. Despite its name, the passive approach still does require a bit of work. The passive, professional-based approach to estimating rent is accomplished by using your team members (described in Chapter 5), specifically real estate agents and property managers. You should call local real estate agents and property managers in the area to ask their opinions on what your unit would rent for. Keep a record of what they tell you, and if an estimate is significantly lower or higher than the majority of the others you received, you should probably remove those data points from your list. If four people say $1,200 per month, one says $900, and one says $1,600, then $1,200 per month is probably the best estimate to go with (unless the individuals who gave you the lower and higher estimates had *very* good reasons to do so). Look at the data you receive from all of the real estate professionals you call and make an educated decision about what you believe is the best estimate based on each person's input.

ALERT

It is important to speak with real estate agents who have specific experience with rentals. Most people are happy to give you their opinion, even if they don't have experience. Not all real estate agents have rental knowledge, so be sure to find one who does.

The active, do-it-yourself approach means that you do the work and research of the real estate professionals. To conduct this research, you should find reputable online sources that can provide rental data for your local area. These may vary depending on your location and when you are reading this book, but three current resources are Rentometer, Zillow, and Facebook Marketplace.

Rentometer

Rentometer is a database of rental data that allows you to enter your property's address into a search bar and get a list of properties in the area and their rental rates. Rentometer calculates your rental rate based on its data and the properties in the area. This site is a great way to get a general idea of what your rent should be, but don't use this as your only source.

Zillow/Facebook Marketplace

Using Zillow and Facebook Marketplace is similar to how you use short-term rental sites to estimate rental rates for your short-term rental. Go on Zillow and/or Facebook Marketplace to find properties similar to yours that are in your area and listed for rent. Once you have a list of these properties, take note of the rental rates. In the professional-based approach, you rely on information you receive from professionals to come to a conclusion. In this do-it-yourself approach, you look up the rental rates yourself. You should also eliminate any rates that are significantly higher or lower than the rest, and do your best to think critically about what the most likely amount is based on the available data. The more data points you have, the better.

ALERT

Zillow is just one of many third-party real estate platforms that can provide relevant data. Trulia, Realtor.com, and Redfin are other popular sites. As long as the site is reputable, choose the one you enjoy using the most and move forward with your analysis.

Combine Methods for Better Accuracy

Many of the listings on third-party sites like Zillow and Facebook Marketplace are from reputable real estate agents who have data backing the rental rates they have chosen, but some of the listings are from individuals who can list their properties for any amount they like without any logical reason. While it is not common for landlords to post inaccurately priced rentals on these sites, it does happen, and you should be aware of how this could impact your estimations.

The data you get *out* of an analysis is only as good as the data you put *in*. If you are unknowingly entering inaccurate information into your analysis because of other landlords making up their own rental rates, that could negatively impact your analysis. If you estimate the rental rate too high for your potential rental unit because of this inaccurate data, it could lead you to purchase a property for a higher price than the numbers truly support. Rather than your house hack reducing your monthly living cost, it could do the opposite.

Just as you can combine multiple house hacking strategies, you can combine the rental rate research methods as well. If you are a new investor, or just a generally skeptical person, who does not mind doing a bit of extra work, you can combine the passive, professional-based approach with the active, do-it-yourself approach. If you want to double-check your own analysis, you can start with the do-it-yourself approach and then move on to the professional-based approach to verify what you have found on your own. This can give you the confidence to rely solely on the active, do-it-yourself approach going forward, if you choose.

Using the Analysis Calculator

Now that you have determined your expected rental income, it is time for you to enter that data into your analysis calculator. You can find this book's deal analysis calculator companion at https://everythinghousehacking.com/house-hacking-calculator. Once you have accessed the calculator, enter your expected rental income in the Monthly Revenue section.

While it is not necessarily common to include other sources of income with house hacking, it is possible. This can include sources like coin-operated laundry, garage access or storage, paid parking, shed storage, and so on. If your house hack provides any opportunities to earn additional revenue each month that is not included in rent, be sure to enter that in the analysis calculator under Other Income in the Monthly Revenue section.

If instead of a long-term strategy you are implementing a short-term rental strategy, you should enter your total expected short-term rental income into the Monthly Revenue section. If you are renting by the room instead of by separate units, you can enter your monthly income per bedroom into the separate cells for units. Unit 1 would be considered Bedroom 1, Unit 2 would be considered Bedroom 2, and so on.

The concept of margin of safety, which was explained in Chapter 4, says that you should purchase an asset at a discount to what you think it's worth to try to cover any mistakes you may have made in your valuation. Margin of safety is arguably more important with short-term rentals than long-term rentals because the rental income amount is harder to estimate. That does not mean you can't and shouldn't apply the concept to your long-term rental analysis as well. If you know you are a bit more risk-averse and conservative, it will serve you well to add a margin of safety to the number you arrived at for your rental income. When implementing a long-term rental strategy, you can also use the margin of safety concept by using a vacancy rate that is slightly higher than what you actually expect. The vacancy rate will be explained in more detail later in this chapter.

ESSENTIAL

Similar to how real estate agents and property managers can assist you in determining your rental rates, they can also help you determine your vacancy rates. If they can't give a specific vacancy rate, you can get an idea by asking questions about how long it takes to rent units like yours during turnovers.

Expense Analysis

Arriving at the correct income at the beginning of your analysis is very important, but so is estimating your expenses accurately. If you start your analysis with an inaccurate rental income number, it is going to be hard to correct that as you work your way down the upside-down pyramid.

The first data points that need to be estimated for your expenses are your acquisition costs, which include the purchase price after repair value (ARV) or expected sale value; closing costs; and repair costs. The deal analysis calculator that is a companion to this book includes an area to input the asking price (https://everythinghousehacking.com/house-hacking-calculator). This allows you to record the difference between the property's asking price and your purchase price so you can look back on your analysis at a later date. Simply record the asking price for the property and the purchase price for which you expect to get the property.

> **ALERT**
>
> You can also insert the amount for which you have the property under contract in the Purchase Price area. However, this is not an ideal process, as you should be running your analysis for the property before you have it under contract. Your analysis tells you if it is a good deal and what price you are willing to acquire it at.

The ARV, or expected sale value, is used in a deal analysis to calculate your estimated internal rate of return (IRR) by acting as the price at which you will sell the property in ten years. There are two approaches to determining this value—conservative and aggressive. In the conservative approach, you would use the value as of today in your analysis. This is estimated by looking at comparable properties in the area to determine the value of the property after you have purchased it and completed renovations, if any. You can ask your real estate agent for assistance in estimating the ARV. This is considered the conservative approach because you are assuming no growth in the value of the property over the next ten years.

The more aggressive approach starts with the same process as the conservative approach. You must first determine the ARV, then apply an annual growth rate to that value to estimate what you think the property will be worth in ten years. For example, if your property has a value today of $100,000 and you expect the value to increase 2 percent every year, on average, for the next ten years, the amount entered for the expected sale value would be approximately $122,000. The IRR calculation would use $122,000, net of any remaining mortgage balance, as the final amount in the tenth year.

The next set of data points you must estimate are in the Financing section; these include your down payment amount, loan interest rate, private mortgage insurance (PMI) percentage, loan term, lender points, and any other financing fees. If you have already received your preapproval from a lender, you can simply take the information from your preapproval documentation and enter it here. If you have not already received a preapproval, you can estimate here what your expected amounts are for your down payment, interest rate, PMI, loan term, and any fees you may need to pay.

Your next considerations in the analysis are your reserves, which include repairs and maintenance, CAPEX, and vacancy, then property taxes, insurance, utilities, landscaping, HOA fees, and any other monthly or annual fees you may have. When it comes to rental property in real estate, reserves are amounts of money put aside each month to cover future one-time expenses. At the time of putting the money aside, the reserves are not an expense; you are simply saving the money. In accounting lingo, reserve savings are considered "non-cash expenses." The items you put money aside for in reserves become actual expenses when you need to use the savings to cover the costs. The other expenses listed are not considered reserves because they are generally recurring on a set basis and require cash to cover the costs.

- Repairs and maintenance refer to small items in your property that need to be fixed or updated due to normal wear and tear.

- CAPEX is similar to repairs and maintenance but involves larger items, such as replacing appliances, putting on a new roof, large painting job, and so on.
- With rental units, vacancy is the amount of time you expect your units to be unoccupied by a renter.

All three of the reserve categories are expressed as a percentage, which is then applied to your gross rental income to determine the dollar amount you should put aside each month or year to cover those estimated future expenses.

When estimating your reserve amounts, there are three approaches you can follow: (1) conservative, (2) aggressive, or (3) do-it-yourself. The conservative and aggressive approaches are both general benchmarks used by investors that can simplify your analysis and make it quicker to complete. The do-it-yourself approach requires that you create your own percentages for each of the three reserve items.

ESSENTIAL

It is important to remember that benchmarks are just that, benchmarks. They work as good rules and starting points for your analysis, but they do not work in every situation. You will probably need to adjust these numbers to better fit your situation. As you gain more analysis experience, you will be able to fine-tune these numbers.

Under the conservative approach, repairs and maintenance are set at 5 percent, CAPEX is set at 10 percent, and the vacancy rate is set at 8 percent. If your rental unit rents for $1,000 per month, based on the conservative benchmarks, you should set aside $50 for repairs and maintenance, $100 for CAPEX, and $80 for vacancy. Under the aggressive approach, repairs and maintenance are set at 2½ percent, CAPEX is set at 5 percent, and the vacancy rate is set at 4 percent. Based on these benchmarks, assuming the same rental income as in the conservative approach, you should set aside $25 for repairs and maintenance, $50 for CAPEX, and $40 for vacancy.

The do-it-yourself approach can be tailored to your specific situation because it requires you to set your own percentages for each of the reserve items. If you know your property is in an area with very strong rental demand, especially for your unit type, you can use an even lower vacancy rate than what the aggressive approach calls for. It can go the other way as well. If your area does not have strong rental demand, or if you are being conservative, you could use an even higher vacancy rate than what is used in the conservative approach.

For CAPEX, as well as repairs and maintenance, the percentages can be adjusted based on the age, quality, size, type, and location of your property. Typically, older properties require more maintenance, in the form of both repairs and CAPEX, unless these items have already been completed by a previous owner. If you are purchasing an older home with common items that need repairs and/or replacing that have not been taken care of—meaning the overall quality is a bit lower than it could be—you should probably increase the percentages you are using for repairs and maintenance and CAPEX, possibly even higher than the conservative amounts. Whereas if you are purchasing a property built in the past decade that has been well maintained, you may be able to use percentages even lower than the aggressive benchmarks.

Considering the size and type of a property when setting reserve percentages is an area of deal analysis that many investors overlook. The reason for this is that they do not realize that the cost of certain items is relatively fixed, regardless of property size and type. For example, the cost of replacing a hot water heater (a CAPEX item) does not tend to vary wildly regardless of the size of your property. If you have more than one hot water heater, you would need to take that into consideration, but the cost of replacing a hot water heater on a 750-square-foot property versus a 2,500-square-foot property is not drastically different. The same can be said for other CAPEX items, such as windows. If your property is a single-family house with ten windows, the cost to replace them is probably not very different than replacing ten windows in a fourplex. This principle can even be applied to replacing a roof. Depending on the structure of your buildings, the cost of replacing a roof on a fourplex does not have to be dramatically different than for a single-family house. It may be slightly more, but you might be surprised at the minimal difference.

The reason this is important is because different property sizes and types generate different amounts of rental income, yet each can have similar CAPEX costs, which can have a big impact on the reserve percentages you need to use in your analysis. For example, if you own a duplex with one rental unit, and you live in the other unit, that produces $1,000 in monthly rental income. Using 10 percent as your CAPEX reserve percentage, you would need to put aside $100 per month. Now assume that instead of a duplex, you have a fourplex with three rental units. Still, each unit provides $1,000 in monthly rental income. But this rental income total is $3,000 per month, and your CAPEX reserve would be $300 per month. Did the cost of replacing your roof just triple too? Most likely not. In many cases, the cost of replacing a roof on a fourplex is not much more than for a duplex. Of course, it can be more expensive; it depends on the configuration and size of the properties, but just because you have more units, and therefore more income, that doesn't mean the cost of CAPEX or repair scales equivalently. If you were to save $100 per month in CAPEX reserves for a duplex, it may be more reasonable to put aside $150 or $200 per month in CAPEX reserves for a similar fourplex, instead of $300 per month.

> **ALERT**
>
> The difference in your reserve amounts could cause you to miss a good deal. The difference of a few hundred dollars per month could cause you to not purchase a property that could make for a great house hack, simply because you analyzed it incorrectly.

Profitability Analysis

It is uncommon to make a true profit when house hacking. That is, more rental income than the entire mortgage payment and expenses. However, it is not uncommon to have your tenant's rent cover more than *your* portion of the mortgage, which reduces your personal housing costs, and is typically the goal of house hacking. It is not impossible to have a true profit; people have done it, but it is certainly not the norm. Profitability analysis in house hacking is when you consider the results of your analysis and determine if the results meet your criteria.

In the companion calculator for this book, you will find a Monthly column and a Year 1 column under the Profit & Loss section. These are the two most common columns investors look at when conducting a profitability analysis. The first column tells you your numbers on a monthly basis, and the second column shows your numbers on an annual basis.

Starting at the top of your upside-down pyramid, you will see your total income, encompassing your rental income and any other secondary income sources. Below that you will see your all-in mortgage amount and any other expenses you may have. The all-in mortgage is the total amount you will be required to pay the bank each month for the property. This includes your principal, interest, taxes, insurance, and PMI. Your other expenses typically include water, sewer, electricity, landscaping, HOA fees, and any other miscellaneous expenses you may have.

QUESTION

Where can I get the expense amounts, such as water, sewer, electricity, landscaping, and HOA fees, for the property I'm analyzing?
You should be able to get amounts for the expense items from the owner who is selling the property. If it is a multifamily property and already a traditional rental that you will be turning into a house hack, the previous landlord should have these amounts readily available for you upon request. If it is a single-family property, it may take a bit longer to get the information together, but it should still be possible.

When you subtract all of your costs from your total rental income, you are left with what is considered your living cost. Living cost is the minimum amount of cash that you will have to pay out of your pocket each month to own the property. It is very important to note that this amount does *not* include any money that should be set aside for reserves. Some house hackers choose not to put any money aside each month for reserves and instead deal with the issues out of their own personal savings if and when the problems arise. This is not the recommended strategy, because if you are buying a house hack for which you can only afford the living cost amount and nothing more, you will not be able to save any money each month, whether it is for reserves or not. If you are not saving money each month, you probably will not have the necessary funds available when something breaks.

Your analysis is not yet complete. Next, you need to subtract your estimated reserve amounts for repairs and maintenance, CAPEX, and vacancy. The resulting number is your adjusted living cost, so called because you are making an adjustment to your original living cost amount to include your reserve amounts. The adjusted living cost is the total amount you would need to take out of your pocket each month to cover your portion of the mortgage and put money aside for reserves.

Profitability Analysis Example

In Chapter 1, you set your goals and expectations, then in Chapter 6, you determined your acceptable financial metrics. Let's walk through a profitability analysis example to illustrate how the wrong reserve percentages can impact your purchasing decisions. For this example, assume you did not want to contribute more than $500 per month toward the mortgage, regardless of the total amount. You find the perfect property to house hack—a triplex that crosses off all your qualitative requirements. Then you start to analyze the property to see if it makes sense quantitatively.

You are relatively conservative, so you use the conservative benchmarks in your analysis for the reserve percentages. Once your analysis is done, you discover that you would have to contribute $650 per month toward the mortgage if you chose to house hack this property. You don't want to give up on the property because it's so perfect qualitatively, so you hire a deal analysis coach to double-check your work. Your coach finds that the percentage you were using for your reserves was too high for a triplex, which caused you to put aside too much each month for reserves. Once the reserve percentages were adjusted to a more accurate number to account for the fact that you were considering a triplex, not a single-family house or duplex, the analysis showed that you only have to contribute $450 per month toward the mortgage! Instead of missing out on a property you loved because of an inaccurate analysis, you are now able to purchase it and start the house hacking wealth supercharger.

ALERT

When you are conducting your profitability analysis to determine whether or not a house hack meets the requirements you determined using the information in Chapters 1 and 6, it is up to you to use either the living cost amount or the adjusted living cost amount. You are encouraged to default to using the adjusted living cost because this will allow you to have reserves set aside for when issues arise, but the choice is yours.

Be As Accurate As Possible

It's true, you could just arbitrarily change the numbers in your analysis to make it work. You could increase your expected rental income, reduce some of your expenses, or change your reserve percentages, even if the changes were inaccurate, just to make it work on paper. However, that will not do you any good. You live in reality, not in the paper of your analysis. Just because you wish for the numbers to be a certain way does not mean they will turn out that way. It is in your best interest to make your analysis as accurate as possible.

This process works very similarly for analyzing traditional rental properties. Instead of the result having to be less than the amount you want to contribute toward the mortgage, you would analyze to determine if the property makes enough profit to satisfy your requirements. With a house hack, you may be willing to pay $500 per month toward the mortgage, but with a traditional rental, you may require $200 per month in profit per unit. The house hacking analysis skills you just learned are transferable to traditional rental analysis and can help you determine if you are missing out on a potentially good rental property by using the wrong reserve percentages.

Review

The last part of your profitability analysis to review is the equity accrued, the reserves saved, and the percentage of mortgage paid. The equity accrued amount is the amount the principal is expected to be paid down in a given year. Reserves saved are the total amount of reserves that are expected to be put aside in that year if the monthly amounts are put aside each month. The percentage of mortgage paid is a metric that shows you how much of the mortgage you are personally paying yourself—the lower the better.

Post–House Hack Analysis

You just learned that many investors do not scale their reserve percentages correctly when analyzing properties with different characteristics. The other most common mistake investors make when analyzing house hack deals is that they do not consider what the numbers will be for the property after they are done house hacking it. If you are planning to sell the property and move on to a new one when you are done house hacking it, then you do not need to do a post–house hack analysis. However, if you are planning on turning your house hack into a traditional rental property once you move out, it is very important to conduct this analysis before purchasing the property, in addition to the house hack analysis you just learned.

It is important to conduct both analyses before purchasing a property because a property may make sense in one scenario but not another. It could be a great house hack property but be a subpar rental, or vice versa. If your main goal is to buy a good rental with a low down payment amount, you may be okay with a mediocre or even subpar house hack on the front end of the deal, as long as it's a great rental on the back end when you move out. Other people may require a much better house hack deal on the front end and accept a lower-quality rental on the back end in exchange. As with many aspects of house hacking, there is no right or wrong here; it is up to you to decide what is right for you and your situation.

As an example, let's assume that one of your house hack requirements is not having to pay more than $500 per month toward the mortgage, and you want to earn at least $300 per month per unit in net cash flow when you move out and turn the property into a traditional rental. You conduct the house hack analysis for a potential property and determine you would only have to pay $400 per month toward the mortgage. This is even better than your requirement, so you decide to move forward with the purchase. After a few months of being in the property, you start to think about your exit strategy. You run a post–house hack analysis and realize the property barely breaks even each month. Never mind meeting your requirement for net cash flow; the property is barely going to be profitable at all. Now you are left with a tough decision.

ESSENTIAL

A saving grace for some investors is that, if you can purchase a great house hack deal, it often makes for a good rental as well. The more you have to pay toward the mortgage each month, the less likely it is to be a good rental, and vice versa.

This issue could have been avoided by conducting a post–house hack analysis before acquiring the property. You could accidentally be drawn into purchasing a property that meets your house hacking requirement but not your rental requirement if you do not conduct both a house hack analysis and a post–house hack analysis.

CHAPTER 9

The Steps to Buying a Property

You've built your team, found your specific area and property and analyzed them, and now you're ready to buy—but how do you do this? In this chapter, you will learn what a mortgage preapproval letter is and how to get one, whom you should get your preapproval letter from, why there is more that goes into getting an offer accepted than just the purchase price, the steps to get a property under contract, what to do after signing the purchase and sale agreement, and the three factors that determine if now is the right time for you to buy real estate.

Mortgage Preapproval

When it comes to purchasing real estate, unless you are paying entirely with cash, one of the first steps is to obtain a preapproval letter from a lender. A mortgage preapproval letter is a document you receive from the financial institution acting as your lender that states how much you are preliminarily approved for. To obtain a preapproval letter, the lender typically requires a set of documents outlining your income and debts, then makes a few calculations to give an approximation of what you are qualified to receive. A full underwriting process is still required to officially approve your loan, which comes much later in the process, but a preapproval letter states that the lender has done its initial due diligence and everything is in order so far for you to qualify for that amount. The process can vary from lender to lender, but preapproval letters are generally valid for ninety days from issuance.

A preapproval letter is one of the first steps in the acquisition process because it needs to be included with your initial offer that your real estate agent submits to the seller or seller's agent. The preapproval letter tells the seller of the property that you have financing in place to purchase their property. Without a preapproval letter with your offer, the seller may not give your offer much consideration, and some sellers may not even accept it.

There are three points during the process of buying a house when people typically get a preapproval letter. There are pros and cons to each. As with many aspects of house hacking, it is completely acceptable to choose the one that fits you and your situation best. The three points at which to acquire a preapproval letter are 1) as soon as you decide you would like to house hack, 2) once you have determined that there are properties available in an area you like, and 3) after you have already found the exact property you would like to acquire.

As Soon As You Decide to House Hack

When you apply for and acquire a preapproval as soon as you decide you want to house hack, you are getting a good start on the acquisition process. You will know up front what documents your lender needs and have plenty of time to get the documents to them, if you are approved or not, and the amount you are approved for (if approved). You will be ready to submit an offer right away if you stumble on to a great property unexpectedly. However, there are potential cons to getting your preapproval this early in the process.

Since preapproval letters are only valid for ninety days with many lenders, you may not be able to find an agent or a property, and get the property under contract, within ninety days of receiving your preapproval letter. If your initial preapproval letter expires, you can apply for a second one, but this will usually cause a second hard inquiry to be added to your credit report. Lenders usually do what is called a "hard pull" of your credit for your first preapproval letter, which adds a hard inquiry to your credit report, and would probably need to do it a second time to provide another preapproval letter. The second hard inquiry ensures that nothing has changed significantly on your credit report over the last ninety days. Two hard inquiries are unlikely to significantly drop your credit score, but it is worth noting that too many hard inquiries can have a negative impact on your score. If you have never obtained a preapproval before, have questionable credit, do not think you can do the preapproval process quickly, or think you may not qualify for a preapproval, the pros of this approach probably outweigh the cons for you.

> **ALERT**
>
> A mortgage is often one of the biggest goals people have when building their credit score. Therefore, unless you need to obtain financing for something else immediately after you purchase your property, it is typically not a big deal if your credit score drops slightly during, or after, this process.

When You're Working with an Agent

Instead of applying for your preapproval letter as soon as you decide to house hack, you could wait until you have found a real estate agent to work with and a property in an area you are happy with. If you choose this approach, there is less chance that your preapproval letter will expire and that you will need multiple hard inquiries on your credit report. However, there is a chance that you *could* stumble upon the perfect property unexpectedly and need a preapproval letter sooner than you can obtain one. This could cause you to miss out on the deal. If you have already been through the preapproval process, have great credit, or feel confident that you can get qualified for a preapproval letter quickly, this may be a more optimal strategy than the previous one.

It Can Change over Time

The approach you choose for obtaining your preapproval letter can change over time. You are not stuck with one approach throughout your house hacking career. If you are a brand-new real estate investor, you will probably go with the first or second option. As you get a bit more experience with real estate transactions, you can go with the second or third option. Your increased experience will teach you what documents are required from lenders, the quality of borrower you are, and how the acquisition process works for buying real estate firsthand. You will learn the turnaround time for obtaining a preapproval letter from your lender and choose the approach that is right for you. The time it takes to obtain a mortgage preapproval letter can vary widely, but with experienced lenders and highly qualified, organized borrowers, you should be able to get a preapproval letter in as little as thirty to sixty minutes. For subpar lenders and borrowers, it can take days or longer.

Getting the Property under Contract

New investors often assume that the sale price is the only factor that matters when sellers are analyzing the offers they have received for their property.

If all else is equal, the sale price is frequently the deciding factor. If two potential buyers submit offers with the same level of quality (chance to close, quality of preapproval letter, and so on) but one has a higher offer price, the higher offer will probably be chosen. However, all else is rarely equal. There is almost always a characteristic or two of an offer that makes it stronger than the others, besides just purchase price.

Many situations can arise during your real estate transaction. They cannot all be covered here, but let's take a look at a few of the most common situations in which price is not the determining factor in the sale of a property: the seller experiencing financial distress and needing a quick close, the seller wanting a low-risk transaction, inheriting the property, legal troubles, or existing property damage.

Seller Experiencing Financial Distress

Financial distress is not always something that can be seen on the outside. Therefore, you might be surprised to learn how many sellers are experiencing some type of financial distress when they are selling their property. Financial distress does not have to be as severe as bankruptcy in the next few days if the property does not sell. It could be more minor circumstances, such as struggling (but able) to pay the mortgage each month or incurring too much credit card debt. If someone is in financial distress, they may be up against a tight timeline to resolve that issue, and selling the property quickly could be more important to them than getting top dollar. Receiving more money from the sale would certainly be beneficial to someone in financial distress, but the extra money is no good to them if they receive it past the deadline for whichever issue they are experiencing.

Wanting a Low-Risk Transaction

Many things can happen in a real estate transaction that could prevent a deal from closing. One of the most common is for the buyer's financing to fall through, which means they would not qualify for the mortgage. In addition to being able to close faster, this is why cash buyers are preferred over buyers who are financing the purchase. There is no financing risk with a cash buyer; therefore, they provide a lower-risk transaction. This dynamic exists not only with cash buyers versus non-cash buyers but also between two non-cash buyers. If one buyer provides a preapproval letter from a lender with a horrible reputation and a bad track record for closing deals, that offer would be seen as less competitive than that of a buyer with a preapproval letter from a strong, reputable lender. Some sellers prefer a low-risk transaction over receiving the most money possible during the sale.

Inheriting the Property

Unfortunately, many people fail to create an easy transfer of their assets to their descendants when they pass away. One of the assets that most commonly causes trouble for those inheriting it is the deceased's home. If you listen to any real estate investing podcasts or speak with wholesalers, you will quickly learn that inherited properties are one of their best deal sources. This is because inheritors usually want the problem gone more than they want to receive the most money possible from the sale. If the inheritor lives close by and the property is in great condition, the sale of the asset is pretty straightforward. However, that is not always the case. The inheritor may live out of state and receive a distressed property that needs work before it is ready to sell. Rather than going through the work and spending the money to get the property into shape to sell for top dollar, many inheritors want an easy transaction to get rid of the problem as quickly as possible.

Legal Troubles

Also high on wholesalers' list of best deal sources is people who are in legal trouble. This trouble can range from needing money to pay lawyers to being incarcerated. There is no shortage of stories from wholesalers who buy properties from individuals serving time in prison. In these cases, the property being sold quickly and easily is often more valuable to the seller than receiving the most money.

Existing Property Damage

If someone wants to receive the most money possible for their property, the property typically needs to be in great condition and have the amenities of newer homes. However, making that a reality for homes that have not been updated in decades can cost tens of thousands of dollars. The average seller usually does not have the money saved to pay for those necessary renovations, or is not willing to invest the money. Also, the seller may not have the money to pay for a major item that needs repair, such as a hot water heater, a furnace, or a roof. This could force them to focus on getting rid of the property quickly rather than trying to receive the most money.

> **ALERT**
>
> While risky, it is possible to waive your contingencies to increase the strength of your offer. If you don't have an easy way to exit the deal without loss, which is what contingencies provide, the seller sees you as more committed than other buyers who have contingencies.

Find the Root Cause of the Sale

The situations just discussed are some of the most common, but they are certainly not the only ones that can come up. Many of these situations are combined as well. You could be purchasing from an investor who is at or near retirement and is looking to get out of real estate. They may not want to deal with fixing the damage at their property or go through a high-risk transaction to get top dollar. Many people, whether they are investors or not, are willing to trade a bit of money for an easier, quicker, and lower-risk transaction.

Unfortunately for buyers, these situations are rarely obvious. If someone is incarcerated, that may be obvious, but if someone inherited a property or is dealing with financial distress, the buyer probably would not know it. When there are multiple offers on a property, try to find out the root cause for the sale. In some cases, the seller does want the highest offer, period, in which case, there is not much you can do other than compete on price. In other cases, if you try to find the root cause of the sale, you can tailor your offer to meet the seller's needs and potentially win the property over someone who may have offered a higher purchase price. You will not always be able to find out the root cause, but there is very little, if any, downside in trying.

ESSENTIAL

If you added a good real estate agent to your team (see Chapter 5), they should be able to guide you through what can be omitted to increase the strength of your offer. They should consider the property, the competitive environment, and your experience to determine what can be waived in your situation.

The market conditions when purchasing your property are going to play a big role in the situations just discussed. They will also play a role in whether or not your offer is accepted right away. As a first-time house hacker, do not be surprised if you receive a counteroffer from the seller after you submit your offer. Real estate transactions often require negotiations—knowing what the seller really cares about can give you a major advantage in your negotiations. After you have submitted your initial offer and gone through counteroffers and negotiations to end up with a deal both sides agree to, you officially have the property under contract.

Conducting Due Diligence and Reviewing Reports

Once you have a property under contract, the clock really starts ticking. That is when everything really starts to move. Unless you have waived your contingencies, which are the items that must be fulfilled satisfactorily or the contract can be canceled without penalty to the buyer, you are now racing against the clock to get everything done before the deadlines. You must conduct your due diligence, conduct any necessary inspections, get an appraisal, potentially negotiate a second time, and work to finalize financing with your lender.

The first step after getting the property under contract is to submit your good-faith deposit, or earnest money, then conduct your inspections. Depending on your location, you may need different types of inspections, but the most common are general home inspections, mold, radon, wood-destroying organisms, and foundation. General home inspections can cover most of those items, but the specifics of your property and/or location could require a more specialized and focused inspection in a particular area. If you have chosen a good agent as part of your team (see Chapter 5), they will guide you through this process and should even handle the scheduling of each of the necessary inspections. Many people choose to be at the property when the inspections are conducted so they can ask questions that come up during the process. Be sure your agent has scheduled the inspections at a convenient time for you, if you choose to attend. In addition to the inspections, you will also need an appraisal. Appraisals are typically ordered from your lender and do not require much work on your end.

Renegotiating

If you are not comfortable with negotiating, a real estate transaction—not just a house hack but any real estate transaction—is certainly going to test you. Once you receive the inspection reports and appraisal, you will probably enter into another negotiation with the seller. Unless you are buying a brand-new build, and even sometimes then, there are issues that show up on the inspection report. You are not required to ask the seller to cover or fix any of the issues that pop up on the report—it can be purely informative for you, if you would like. However, many buyers do ask the seller to cover or fix at least some of the issues on the inspection reports, and that is when you would need to reenter into negotiation.

Part of this second negotiation can include a discussion of the appraisal as well. Typically, if the appraisal amount is at or above the purchase price, there is no need to discuss it. However, if the appraisal comes in lower than the purchase price, there needs to be a discussion between the buyer and seller, and potentially a negotiation to lower the price that was agreed upon because your lender is not going to finance the purchase of a property for more than it is worth.

If you have the cash available and choose to cover the difference between the purchase price and appraisal amount to satisfy your lender's loan-to-value requirements, that is an option that would allow you to avoid renegotiating with the seller. But most house hackers choose to house hack because they are early in their wealth-building journey and/or do not have a lot of capital, so covering the difference may not be viable for you. This gap between purchase price and appraised value can give you an advantage when negotiating because appraisals are universal for a property; they do not change based on the buyer. A property is worth what the property is worth, regardless of who is buying it. Therefore, the seller is going to run into the same issue with any buyer who wants to purchase that property. Some buyers may be willing to cover the difference with cash, but the seller may have mentally written off this property as sold and may not want to go through the entire process again with a new buyer. Similar to the reasons why price is not always the determining factor, the seller may prefer to just close the deal rather than trying to find a buyer to cover the difference.

Watch Your Dates

At this point in the process, you are still racing against the clock. As part of the purchase and sale agreement, your agent has listed a timeline outlining when certain tasks will be completed, such as the inspection, the appraisal, and obtaining final financing. If you have not waived your contingencies for these items, specifically the inspections and appraisals, you will need to have those items completed *and* complete any negotiations regarding them before the deadlines listed in the purchase and sales agreement in order to avoid losing your earnest money. If you are not going to meet these deadlines, you can request an extension from the seller so you do not lose your earnest money, but they are not required to provide you with one.

ALERT

The important dates in a real estate transaction can easily get buried with all the documentation that gets exchanged. To ensure no date is missed or forgotten, create a timeline with all the important dates (you can find a timeline tracker at https://everythinghousehacking.com/timeline-tracker) or add them into your phone's calendar with reminders.

Contingencies

In a real estate transaction, contingencies allow you to back out of a transaction without penalty, such as losing your earnest money, if certain processes do not get completed satisfactorily and you back out before the deadline. Common contingencies are inspections, appraisals, current home sale, and financing. Earnest money, also known as a good-faith deposit, is a sum of money that the buyer puts into escrow immediately after getting the property under contract to show they are serious about buying the property. This shows that the buyer is serious because the money is considered "at-risk capital." It is at risk because if you back out of the transaction *after* your contingency deadlines have passed, you will forfeit your entire earnest money deposit. However, if something comes back in the inspection report that you are unhappy with or you cannot come to an agreement with the seller to remediate that issue, you can back out of the deal before your inspection contingency deadline and still receive your full earnest money deposit. When everything goes smoothly in a transaction and closes as intended, the earnest money deposit is applied toward your down payment amount.

Once you have concluded any negotiations with the seller after receiving the inspection and appraisal reports, you are now locked in on that purchase price and deal terms while you wait for your lender to finalize its underwriting and provide the "clear-to-close." A "clear-to-close" is simply the official approval from your lender that the closing, or transfer of a property's ownership, is allowed to be conducted.

Final Step: Closing

As you wait for your clear-to-close, there is not much for you, the buyer, to do in this transaction other than wait for your lender to do their job and to assist them with any additional documentation or information they may need. It is wise to stay on top of your lender and check in with them frequently, but mainly it is up to them to finish their underwriting. The final contingency remaining is usually your financial contingency, which means you can still receive your full earnest money deposit back if you are unable to obtain financing before the deadline set as part of your purchase and sales agreement. By checking in with your lender frequently, you decrease your odds of missing the financial contingency deadline and possibly losing your earnest money deposit.

If you are selling the property you currently live in, you will need to go through all the steps just discussed, but as the seller instead of the buyer. If you are moving out of an apartment or another property that you do not own, you will need to complete the necessary tasks to be prepared for the move.

Once you have received the clear-to-close from your lender, your real estate agent should schedule a final walk-through of the property for the day of closing. The final walk-through can be conducted any time, but it is recommended to schedule it as close to closing as possible. It is ideal to go directly from the walk-through to closing. A final walk-through allows you to see the property one last time before acquiring it to verify and sign off that nothing has changed since the inspections. Once the inspections are completed, the buyer rarely sees the property again until the final walk-through, which can be anywhere from a few days for cash buyers to thirty or more days for buyers with financing. A lot of negative things can happen in a thirty-day time frame. There is no shortage of horror stories about significant problems occurring at the property between inspections and the final walk-through. For example, if the property is in an area where the temperature drops significantly, the pipes might freeze, then burst and flood the property. This may sound a bit dramatic, but it happens far more frequently than you may realize.

After the final walk-through, it is time to sign more papers than you have probably ever signed before in one sitting. It's time for closing. The location of your closing will probably take place at a lawyer's office or in a title company's office. Be sure to bring the required forms and documentation with you to the closing. A lawyer or title agent will walk you through the documentation, and you will sign each document. Once this is done, the closing is finished and you nearly own the property. You will have official ownership of the property and receive the keys once the deed has been recorded at the local city, town, or county office.

When Is the Right Time to Buy?

Now that you know all the steps to find and buy your house hack, you may be wondering *when* you should do all of this. There are three factors to consider when determining if the time is right to buy your house hack. The first is your personal life situation, the second is your financial situation, and the third is the overall health and timing of the markets.

Your Personal Life

Buying any real estate property and moving is no easy task. House hacking can make the process slightly more difficult because you have to make some compromises with your living situation and also start managing tenants. Depending on what is going on in your life, it may be the perfect time to start house hacking, or it may not be quite the right time. If you just started a brand-new job that is demanding and requires a lot of time and attention, or if you just had a baby or are expecting, right now might not be the best time to start. It may make more sense for you to be a bit more settled into your job and/or family life before taking on a big move and new endeavor.

Do not, however, let yourself make excuses and postpone implementing the house hacking strategy because of minor hurdles. As you learned in previous chapters, house hacking takes hard work and sacrifice. If you wait until the absolute perfect time to start, you may never make the leap. The decision is yours, but do not let yourself fall comfortably into complacency. Real change comes when you push your boundaries and challenge yourself.

Your Financial Situation

In addition to your personal life being fairly settled, your personal finances must also be in good shape before you house hack. The two components of your personal finances that you need to look at are your credit and the amount of cash you have saved. You will learn how to get your credit in order in Chapter 10, but for now, understand that your credit must be good enough to allow you to qualify for the mortgage. The amount of cash you need to be ready to house hack is going to vary from person to person and from deal to deal. One person may buy a house hack that needs immediate repairs for $750,000 with 5 percent down and no seller credits. That person is going to need more readily available cash than someone who buys a property that is move-in ready for $250,000 with 3½ percent down and $10,000 in seller credits.

> **FACT**
>
> A seller credit is when the property seller gives cash back to the buyer at closing, generally in the form of covering part or all of the buyer's closing costs. Seller credits are a way to reduce the amount of cash a buyer needs to buy the property.

In the first example, the buyer would need $37,500 just for the down payment, plus a few thousand dollars for closing costs and enough to cover the necessary repairs, say, $10,000. The second buyer would only need $8,750 for the down payment, has covered their entire closing costs using a seller credit, and does not need any money for repairs because the house is move-in ready. Those are the minimum amounts that the buyers would need to close on their respective properties, but neither example includes any amount for reserves.

It is highly recommended that you put aside money in reserves when buying your property. The buyer in the second example could theoretically buy their property with only $8,750, but if they only have $8,751 saved, then it is not a prudent financial decision to buy that property yet. Murphy's law says that "anything that can go wrong will go wrong," and if you talk to enough real estate investors, you will see this is true in real estate. Of course, there is no guarantee something bad will happen, but there have been many times when the hot water heater broke a few days after the buyer moved in, or the furnace stopped working, or a major appliance broke. With a house hack, you also have the risk of your tenants not paying their rent. If that happens, your mortgage payment is still due—you must cover it yourself.

If you do not have any money remaining after acquiring the property, you are in a weak financial position and will likely struggle to cover any unexpected issues that come up. Similar to the reserve percentages in your deal analysis, the exact amount you should set aside for reserves initially when buying the property depends on many factors and varies in each situation. Start by understanding the quality and condition of the property you're buying, then choose a reserve amount you are comfortable with given your situation's potential risks.

ESSENTIAL

A rule for your initial reserve amount is one to three times the monthly rent you expect to receive from your tenants, and/or the amount it would cost to fix or replace a small- to medium-sized CAPEX item, such as a hot water heater or large appliance.

Overall Health of the Real Estate Market

The third factor to consider when determining if the time is right to buy your house hack is the overall health and timing of the real estate market. It is human nature to worry that you will invest at the wrong time, so you wait until the time is "right." For some odd reason, despite numerous studies showing otherwise, people think they can time capital markets, whether it be the stock market or real estate. It is commonly accepted that years of advanced education are required to enter certain fields, such as medicine, law, engineering, and accounting. Yet individual investors think they can wake up one day, with no or limited education or experience, and go toe-to-toe with those who have dedicated their entire lives to this field.

No matter how many studies show there is no reliable way to time the market, or how many of the world's best investors repeatedly warn that it is not possible even for them, people *still* attempt to do it, to their detriment. The reality is, there is no perfect time to buy real estate. The perfect moment only exists in hindsight.

It is possible to purchase a property tomorrow at the peak of your market, only for things to crash the very next day. It is also possible to buy at levels that seem elevated in the moment, when considered historically, but the market remains stable for many years to follow and you do very well. You can review data to try to predict what's to come, but you will never know for certain. You will never know in the present moment when is the perfect time to buy real estate.

Many new investors say they will wait for a crash to start buying real estate. They wait until prices come down a bit, then they get started. If this has been or is your philosophy, you are challenged to consider this: If you are not willing to invest in the best of times, when capital is plentiful and obtaining financing is as easy as it has ever been, why do you think you should invest in the worst of times, when money is hard to come by and financing is significantly harder to obtain? When there is blood in the streets and many experienced investors are running the other way, why do you think you, a new and inexperienced investor, will have the discipline and abilities to go against the crowd and invest? From a financial institution's perspective, when they have massively tightened their lending standards and are being very selective with whom they will lend to, why would they choose to lend to someone who has no real estate experience when times are tough?

Let's say you are among the crowd who is waiting for a crash to start investing. After waiting for years, the market crash you expected finally comes. You say to yourself, "Yes! I knew it!" only to realize you missed out on years and years of gains in the meantime. Because the markets are crashing, opportunities are plentiful and there are many potential properties to buy. But, because markets are crashing, capital is hard to come by and you can't get financing—banks slow or even stop lending. Maybe you lose your job. Due to the hard times, you tell yourself you'll get started when things improve. You are psychologically scarred from this crash, so despite improving markets, you continue to nervously wait on the sidelines. By the time you're ready to start, the markets are considered elevated again and you fall into the same old philosophy you had previously: "I'll invest when the market crashes." More years pass, and you never got started. Do you see how this can quickly become a self-fulfilling and vicious cycle?

ALERT

Two of the best ways to reduce your nervousness or anxiety about buying real estate are to fully understand and be well educated on what you're doing, and making sure you are well capitalized with enough in reserves. Nervousness and anxiety stem from not knowing what you're doing and not being prepared to weather a potential storm.

There is no perfect time to buy real estate. Of the three factors that determine if now is the right time, there are two you can control and one you cannot. Focus on and perfect what you *can* control and let the rest be. If you have done the legwork of getting educated and are sure you are buying a good deal that is sustainable, it's always the right time to buy real estate. The two biggest risks are never getting started and the regret that ensues.

CHAPTER 10

Financing Your House Hack

You've done all the work to find the property you'd like to house hack, and now it's time to buy it. You probably don't have the cash just sitting in the bank, so you are going to need to obtain financing through a mortgage. In this chapter, you will learn the types of institutions available to finance your house hack, the pros and cons of each and which may be best for your situation, the types of loan products offered by each financial institution, what underwriting is and what lenders are looking for, and how to get your credit in order to potentially save hundreds of thousands of dollars.

Types of Financial Institutions

Many people simply use the financial institution their parents or grandparents use. Maybe your parents helped you set up your first account when you were a kid, and you have just never switched, or, when it was time to open your account, you asked your family members for recommendations and chose the institution they use. However you ended up at the current financial institution you use, there are probably other types you may not be familiar with that might be beneficial for your house hack.

Interacting with your money via checking or savings accounts with a financial institution is typically referred to as "banking." The verb used to describe these financial actions is related to banks because they were the main type of financial institution until fairly recently. There were not many other types of financial institutions, so when you conducted financial activities with a bank, the term used was *banking*.

FACT

The first bank in the United States was founded in 1791, and one of the world's first banks as they are known today was founded in 1624, but records for it can be traced back even further to 1472.

There are two major types of banks in the United States today—national and local banks. Within these two types, there are subcategories, such as retail, commercial, investment, online, and community development. National and local banks operate similarly but have different areas and scales in which they operate. National banks are typically much larger than local banks and have a presence across the entire United States, whereas a local bank is probably focused in one or a few smaller regions. Due to their size and scale, national banks often have slightly better technology offerings and more resources for customers, but that does not necessarily mean that they have the best rates for interest-bearing accounts or loan products.

Retail, Commercial, and Investment Banks

Retail banks are the type of bank you are probably most familiar with. They offer traditional bank products to consumers, such as checking and savings accounts, auto loans, credit cards, and more. Commercial banks offer similar products to those of retail banks but to businesses and legal entities rather than individual consumers, in addition to specialty products and services for business entities. Commercial operations can be stand-alone entities that are entire commercial banks, or there can be commercial divisions or departments within a larger institution. Investment banks are focused on providing investment products and services to both individual and commercial clients, instead of focusing on everyday savings, checking, and credit products like other types of banks.

Online and Community Development Banks

Online banks operate very similarly to retail and commercial banks, depending on the bank's focus, but they are purely online without any physical branch locations. Typically, online banks offer similar products and services to retail and commercial banks, but they do not offer a location that their customers can go to in person to get assistance. Community development banks are more of a specialty organization, as they are not designed to serve the entire public but rather focus on providing financial services to underserved communities. Community development banks are often subsidized or supported by the federal government.

> **ALERT**
>
> Online banks are relatively new compared to traditional brick-and-mortar banks, but they have done a good job of making the user experience as seamless as possible. The reduced overhead and fixed costs that online banks have typically translate into lower fees, lower loan interest rates, and higher savings accounts interest rates.

Credit Unions

The term "banking" had been used in the United States for over one hundred years, and the first US credit union was established in April of 1909. Even though people may refer to their financial activity with a credit union as doing their "banking," credit unions are not a bank—they are actually quite different than the banks just described. Banks are owned by public or private shareholders, and banks have customers. Credit unions do not have customers; they have members who own the credit union, and they are not-for-profit organizations. You might be thinking, "Why does this relatively minor distinction between what they call their clients matter?" That is a great question because it *does* matter and is not common knowledge. When an organization has shareholders, whether it be a bank or another type of corporation, the ultimate goal is to create value for its shareholders, typically in the form of increasing the total value of the organization or providing its shareholders with cash flow. Banks usually generate income from interest rate spreads and fees they charge their customers, which can include overdraft fees, transaction fees, certified check fees, and everything in between.

ESSENTIAL

An interest rate spread is the difference between how much the bank pays their customers on their deposits in the form of interest and how much the customers pay the bank in interest on their loans.

American investor and real estate attorney Charlie Munger famously talked about the power of incentives. He has said, "Never, ever, think about something else when you should be thinking about the power of incentives." If you consider just this quote, you can see why there is a misalignment of incentives with banks that does not exist with credit unions.

If banks have shareholders and the ultimate goal of providing value to their shareholders by charging their customers fees and profiting off interest rate spreads, what does that make their incentives? Are they incentivized to charge their customers no or low fees, provide high interest rates on savings accounts, and charge the lowest rates possible on loan products? Of course not. That would result in the least revenue for the bank and therefore is not aligned with their incentives. A bank's incentives often do not provide the best products and services to its end customers—you.

ALERT

People with a great deal of money or businesses that require special services are often better served by traditional banks than credit unions, because these banks are large enough to create more niche products and services to handle their needs.

Since credit unions are not-for-profit organizations and are owned by their members—which simply means anyone who has money on deposit with them—the incentive structure is entirely different than with banks. As not-for-profit organizations, credit unions are not set up to maximize profitability, and any profitability they do have is reinvested into the credit union in the form of lower fees, high savings account rates, lower loan interest rates, technological improvements, and even better benefits for their employees. Also, since the members *are* the owners, credit unions are not incentivized to charge fees to their members to give to owners—they would be charging themselves. All of this leads to an incentive structure for credit unions that significantly benefits its members more than a bank's incentive structures.

This is not to say that credit unions do not charge fees or have zero-interest rate loans, nor does this mean that credit unions are better than banks in every aspect. Credit unions still have employees and operating costs to cover, so there must be a form of sustainable revenue. Credit unions are also typically much smaller than banks, which can mean that banks have more resources at their disposal to provide a wider selection of products and services, as well as better technology platforms. Banks also have more physical locations than do credit unions.

Hard Money Lender

Another financial institution you will come across in your real estate investing journey is a hard money lender. Hard money lenders typically are not banks and therefore do not offer traditional banking products or services like checking and savings accounts. Instead, hard money lenders provide short-term, high-interest-rate loans to real estate investors to get their projects completed. In the case of a real estate project where a large rehab is needed, you might use a hard money lender to complete the project instead of your own money or a traditional lender.

If you were to use only your own money, you would have to fund 100 percent of the project. However, if you use a hard money lender, you would typically fund just 20–25 percent of the purchase and rehab. Hard money lenders are also often used in place of traditional lenders when doing large rehab projects because traditional loan products cannot be used for homes that are not move-in ready. Once a project is completed, you can sell it and use the proceeds to pay off the hard money lender, or you can finance with a traditional loan product and use those proceeds to pay off the hard money lender.

Using a hard money lender is a bit more of a complex strategy and is often not used until an investor has more experience. Since many house hackers are relatively new or brand-new to real estate investing, hard money lenders may not be the best option. However, this strategy could come into play if you are house hacking a property that needs a large rehab. If you do your due diligence up front, understand the ins and outs of hard money lenders, have a firm grasp on the rehab, and create an exit plan to refinance with a traditional lender, you may be able to use a hard money loan to purchase a house hack with significant equity built in.

Private Lenders

Private lenders, also known as private money, are similar to hard money lenders, but they can act in a similar capacity to traditional lenders as well. Private lenders can also be the seller from which you are buying your property. An individual with enough capital to do so can lend their money to another real estate investor to complete a large rehab project, in the exact same way a hard money lender would. Instead of the real estate investor receiving the money from a company, they would receive it from one or several individuals from their own personal savings. In this capacity, the private lender is still offering a short-term, high-interest loan. The private lender sees this as their own investment, which is considered a debt investment.

> **FACT**
>
> Rather than investing their savings in the stock market, bonds, real estate syndications, their own active real estate investments, or any other asset, the private lender chooses to lend that money as private funds to other real estate investors in order to earn a passive return that is backed by a hard (tangible) asset.

The shorter-term loans just discussed work well for some private lenders because they provide higher rates of return and get the money back to the lender more quickly. However, these lenders will need to continue putting that money into new projects to keep earning interest. Some private lenders prefer to provide longer-term loans, similar to traditional financing loans. Hard money loans, whether from a company or a private lender, are typically twelve months or less in length, whereas longer-term loans can be five, ten, fifteen, twenty, or more years in length—just like a traditional mortgage loan product. The difference between traditional mortgage loan products and private lenders offering long-term loans is that the interest rate is generally quite a bit higher from private lenders than from traditional lenders.

Seller Financing

The private lender's capital does not have to be in the form of cash, as in the previous two examples. Instead, it can be in the form of equity. If you are purchasing a property from someone who owns their property outright with no mortgage, they could use their equity in the property to finance the property to you. Instead of going to a traditional lender and obtaining a mortgage, the seller can be the bank for you. This is known as using seller financing, a form of private money, with the seller acting as the private lender. With seller financing, the buyer pays the monthly mortgage payment to the seller, who is the lender in this case, instead of to a traditional financial institution. Using seller financing is a bit complex, but not quite as complex as using hard money loans. Imagine a scale from left to right, with the easiest financing strategies on the left to the hardest on the right. Of the examples you have learned in this book, traditional financing is farthest to the left, hard money loans are the farthest to the right, and seller financing is somewhere in the middle.

ALERT

You might be wondering why a seller would ever use seller financing, but it can actually be quite beneficial. It can provide the seller with consistent cash flow for a period, it often has positive tax implications for the seller, and the seller can sometimes even get a higher sale price by offering seller financing.

Pros and Cons

The biggest benefit of these untraditional forms of financing is their flexibility. With traditional lenders and their loan products, you have to fit into a figurative box and fulfill each item on the lender's very strict and defined list of criteria. With hard money lenders and private money lenders, you have far more flexibility. A hard money lender provides more flexibility than a traditional lender but less than a private lender. The hard money lending company probably has defined terms and a process that you must also abide by. Despite that, it is still more flexible than traditional lenders. Private money lenders can have ultimate flexibility. This does not mean that every private money lender will give you the exact terms and structure you'd like, but the possibility exists. If you are looking for specific terms and structure, you need to find a private money lender that will agree to your requirements. Obtaining financing from a private money lender is a negotiation, just like trying to purchase a property. You present your side, they present theirs, and you negotiate until you come to terms or decide to walk away. With traditional lenders, you either agree to what they say, or you do not use them.

Despite its rigidity and drawbacks, traditional financing is the best option for house hacking. If you have a stable job with W-2 income and can satisfy the rest of a traditional lender's requirements, that is most likely the best path for you. However, if you cannot fit into the traditional lender's box or satisfy all their requirements, you do not have to give up—there are other options for you.

Types of Loans

Within the financial institutions you learned about in the previous section, there are multiple types of loan products that each one offers. Traditional lenders can offer Federal Housing Administration (FHA) loans; conventional mortgages; and 203k, USDA, and Veterans Affairs (VA) loans. Lenders can offer all of these loan products, but they are not required to. They can specialize in and only offer one type, they can choose a few, or they can offer them all—it varies from lender to lender.

> **ESSENTIAL**
>
> FHA loans are often confused with first-time home buyer loans because of the loan's structure and requirements, and the fact that many first-time home buyers use these loans. However, just because many first-time home buyers use the loans does not mean that they are exclusively first-time home buyer loans. In fact, you can use an FHA loan after you have already purchased many real estate properties.

FHA Loans

Decades ago, conventional loans required a large down payment percentage, usually 20 percent, to purchase a home, which made it difficult for first-time home buyers to purchase a property. To combat this, the Federal Housing Administration, with the Department of Housing and Urban

Development (HUD), created the FHA loan program that required much lower down payment amounts, lower closing costs, and easier credit requirements. Instead of borrowers having to put 20 percent down, pay high closing costs, and needing great credit to purchase a home using conventional financing, FHA loans allow them to put just 3½ percent down, with lower closing costs and worse credit. This led to many young and first-time home buyers using FHA loans, and subsequently confusing them with first-time home buyer loans.

Conventional loans have stricter underwriting and credit requirements than FHA loans, but they offer more flexibility on the condition of the house. FHA loans have strict requirements on the condition of the property, and you must pass various FHA-specific inspections before the lender provides its clear-to-close. The items on FHA inspections can be as small as chipping paint on windows or decks and missing railings on stairs. In general, conventional financing is less strict on the condition of the property and requires only that it is habitable at the time of closing. The items mentioned for FHA inspections would not be an issue for closing a conventional loan, but would need to be addressed before closing with an FHA loan. Both loans typically offer some of the lowest interest rates you can get on a mortgage loan product.

Rehab Loan (203K Loan)

The FHA also offers the 203k loan program, which is often referred to as the "rehab loan." It is called the rehab loan because it allows borrowers to purchase a fixer-upper and even finance some or all of the rehab costs. The standard FHA loan has strict requirements about the property's condition at closing, whereas the FHA 203k loan removes those requirements. With the FHA 203k loan, the loan amount can cover the purchase price and up to $30,000 in rehab costs, while only requiring 3½ percent down. Let's look at a specific example.

If you purchase a house for $200,000 that needs $30,000 worth of rehab, your all-in cost would be $230,000. Instead of obtaining a loan for $200,000, with 3½ percent down, then funding the $30,000 rehab yourself, you can use an FHA 203k loan and put 3½ percent down on the $230,000 amount. In the first scenario, you would need $7,000 for the 3½ percent down, plus $30,000 for the rehab, for a total of $37,000. In the second scenario, using an FHA 203k loan, you would only need $8,050.

ALERT

In addition to standard FHA 203k loans, there is also an FHA Limited 203k loan. The FHA Limited 203k loan differs from the standard loan in that it is only allowed to do "limited" repairs, mostly cosmetic items, such as kitchen and bathroom remodels, appliance replacement, carpet/flooring installation, and paint jobs. You can take on more extensive rehabs with the standard FHA 203k loans.

These two construction loans are part of the FHA program, which means they both have similar underwriting requirements and loan characteristics, such as up-front mortgage insurance premiums and PMI that lasts for the life of the loan. There is a similar loan product that is conventional, called the Fannie Mae HomeStyle mortgage. This works like an FHA 203k loan, but it has a 5 percent down payment requirement instead of 3½ percent, it does not have the up-front mortgage insurance premium, and mortgage insurance can be removed once you have 22 percent equity in the property.

VA Loans

Another popular loan product is the Veterans Affairs (VA) loan. You must be a service member, veteran, or qualified surviving spouse to use these loans, but if you are eligible, they are one of the best loan products available. These loans are similar to FHA loans in how they are structured on the back end with guarantees. FHA loans are provided by independent, private lenders and are insured and guaranteed by the Federal Housing Administration and HUD. VA loans are also provided by independent, private lenders and are insured and guaranteed by Veterans Affairs. This structural difference is important to understand because you must still go through lenders to obtain these mortgages—you are not going directly to the FHA, HUD, or VA.

VA loans are one of the best loan products because they do not require down payments, which is often one of the largest obstacles for potential home buyers, yet they do not require PMI. If you are a veteran looking to house hack and you use a VA loan, you can buy your property with no down payment. As long as you abide by the rules and fine print of your specific loan, you could even turn the property into a rental after living there for twelve months—that means you could get a rental property for zero dollars down.

If you put less than 20 percent down using an FHA or conventional loan, you will be required to pay for PMI. However, that is not the case with VA loans—no PMI is required. VA loans also have some of the lowest closing costs of all mortgage products while maintaining competitively low interest rates similar to FHA and conventional loan products. The benefits of a VA loan are for a lifetime, and you can use it more than once. Not everyone is going to be eligible for this loan product, but if you are, it's a great option to consider and likely your best choice.

USDA Loans

Similar to both the FHA and VA loans, there are loan programs offered through another government agency—the US Department of Agriculture (USDA). FHA and VA loan programs can change their requirements and/or offerings from time to time, but there haven't been any *major* changes to these programs lately. They are also relatively straightforward. USDA loan programs, on the other hand, are ever-changing and significantly more complex. Rather than memorizing or learning all the intricacies of the current USDA loan programs, it is enough to know that USDA loan products exist. You can research the specifics of the available loan programs, then decide if one of them is a good fit for you.

Creative Financing

The loan programs you just learned about all fall under the category of "traditional financing." In the Types of Financial Institutions section, you learned about hard money and private money lenders as well as their respective loans. These are considered to be in the "creative financing" category and are additional options to traditional financing options.

You might be thinking, "I'm just going to put 3½ percent down and buy a duplex; why do I need to know about all of these other loan products?" That is a fair question. The reality is that you never know when you may need this information. Maybe your current situation and the property you want to buy fit perfectly into the theoretical FHA loan requirement box. But what about your second property? Or your third? What if you want to buy a traditional rental after or during your house hack?

Most of the people reading this book will fall into the traditional financing category, but not everyone. This information helps those who may need to take a more creative route. You may not need this information right now, but it could apply to your future situation.

> **ESSENTIAL**
>
> You cannot connect the dots looking forward, only looking back. You can only become a better investor by learning more about real estate investing and all the avenues available. Risk and stress come from not knowing what you are doing—the more you know, the less risk and stress you have.

Financial Institutions' Underwriting Process

When you apply for a mortgage, you are asked numerous questions that seem to never end and have to submit a huge list of documents to your lender, specifically your loan processor. Then your loan processor tells you they are submitting all of your information and documentation to "underwriting." Unless you have worked in the mortgage industry or spent time studying it, you probably have no idea what underwriting means, and you might be surprised that you are not all set. You do have a preapproval after all, don't you? Unfortunately, the preapproval letter you received does *not* mean you are going to be granted the mortgage. The preapproval simply tells you that, based on the initial information and documentation you have provided, everything looks satisfactory.

Once your information and documentation go to underwriting, the mortgage underwriter goes over your information, documentation, and the transaction details in significantly more detail. Most mortgage underwriters are people, but there are automated underwriting programs that can do the majority of this process automatically. Underwriters' main goal is to assess the risk of providing you with a mortgage. To do this, they review your income, mortgage loan amount, total assets, total debts, debt-to-income (DTI) ratio, credit score, credit report, and employment history. They will also look at the appraisal and conduct a title search.

DTI Ratio

The most important factor in arriving at their main decision—your riskiness as a borrower—is to determine if you can afford the loan. This is simple but not easy; there is a lot that goes into it. Underwriters will look at your gross income, from your W-2 job for most people, your monthly debt payments from liabilities such as car loans and student loans, and the expected monthly mortgage payment if you are approved. These numbers are put into a formula to calculate your DTI ratio, of which there are two—front-end DTI and back-end DTI.

Your front-end DTI is your DTI ratio *before* you obtain the mortgage. This is calculated by adding up all of your monthly debt payments and dividing that number by your total monthly gross income, without including the mortgage you are trying to obtain. Your back-end DTI is computed similarly to the front-end DTI, except that it *does* include the mortgage you are trying to obtain.

Many mortgage companies are looking for a front-end DTI ratio in the range of 40–45 percent, with the back-end DTI ratio not exceeding 50 percent. These ranges do vary from lender to lender and depend on your credit score and report. A borrower with a very strong credit history and high credit score is probably going to be allowed a higher DTI ratio than someone with a worse credit history and lower credit score, all else being equal.

Not only does your DTI have to fit certain requirements; it also needs to be sustainable. If you have a very low front- and back-end DTI today but your job is very unstable or you have a weak job history, these factors would be looked upon unfavorably by the underwriter. To determine the stability of your job, the underwriter and/or lender may consider the industry you are in and its prospects. For your job history, they will look at how often you change jobs and if you are changing job types or industries frequently. You will be asked how long you have been in your current role, and if you have not been there long, you will be asked about your previous role(s) to determine if you are jumping around. Constant shifting of job types and industries is seen as a sign of risk for lenders, as it can indicate instability.

The underwriter is also interested in your total assets, mainly your liquid assets. Liquid assets are items that can easily be converted into cash, which is why the underwriter is interested in them. If you run into financial trouble like a job loss or overextending on monthly loan payments, the lender wants to know that you have liquid assets that you could convert to cash to satisfy their loan payments.

Credit Score

With many loan products, such as car loans, credit cards, and mortgages, your credit score not only plays a role in determining if you are going to be approved; it also determines your interest rate. As an example, mortgage programs often have a minimum credit score requirement. Let's say the minimum credit score requirement is 650. Many borrowers with scores below that are instantly denied, regardless of how impressive the rest of their application is. The higher your score is above 650, the better chance you have of being approved and the lower interest rate you can receive. Someone with an 800 credit score has a better chance of being approved than someone squeaking by with a 650. Likewise, someone with an 800 credit score will receive a lower interest rate than someone with a 650. Interest rates are typically given based on which bracket your credit score falls into. As an example, one bracket may be between 650 and 700, then 701 to 750, and so on, with each bracket having a corresponding interest rate.

Fannie Mae and Freddie Mac

Many of the most common mortgage loan products are backed by two companies created by Congress that work under a congressional charter today—Fannie Mae and Freddie Mac. The goal of these entities is to provide stability and liquidity to the mortgage markets by packing loans together into mortgage-backed securities (MBS) and selling them to investors. To put it simply, many of the lenders you will work with only originate the loan and potentially service it; they do not actually own the loan. The lender will do all the up-front work to originate the loan, then sell the loan to Fannie Mae or Freddie Mac. In some instances, the lender who originated the loan will retain servicing, but sometimes that is transferred as well.

ALERT

Mortgage servicing is simply when a company processes and handles the loan payments, documentation, loan changes, tax forms, and the like. The servicing can be done by the company that owns the loan, or it can be retained by a company that has already sold off the mortgage.

This is important to understand because much of the underwriting process is already defined for the lenders. Fannie Mae and Freddie Mac have a very defined set of criteria that borrowers must meet and that is passed on to the lender who is originating the loan. Fannie Mae and Freddie Mac get the funding for the loans from selling them as MBSs to investors. The investors are essentially funding the mortgages, but they are spreading their risk among many mortgages through the MBS, rather than just one mortgage, like a private lender might do. For Fannie Mae or Freddie Mac to package the loans into the MBS to sell to investors, the borrowers have to meet their criteria. If Fannie Mae or Freddie Mac can't package the loans into the MBS, they are not going to acquire, or buy, the loans from the original lender. Then, the original lender will be stuck with the loans, which is usually not the desired outcome. Therefore, the lenders have to ensure all of the loans they originate meet or exceed Fannie Mae's or Freddie Mac's criteria. Not all loans are considered agency debt, which simply means it is part of a program offered by Fannie Mae, Freddie Mac, or another government agency, but those that are follow the process just described. As you can probably imagine, this is a relatively simple overview of a very complex financial system. It does not describe every detail of the process, but it is important to at least have a basic understanding of how it works. By understanding this process, you can better prepare for the mortgage process.

FACT

Some lenders specifically choose to keep a portion of the loans on their balance sheets, while others choose to sell off all of them. There are also lenders, known as "portfolio lenders," who lend their own money, not government funds.

Getting Your Credit In Order

On a car loan, where the term of the loan is pretty short, usually between three and six years, and the amount is relatively small, the interest rate is not *as* important as it is with a house loan. It is important, but not quite as much as a thirty-year mortgage that can be hundreds of thousands of dollars. For example, a car loan of $25,000 for five years at an interest rate of 2 percent would require you to pay a total of just about $1,300 in interest. If you doubled the interest rate, to 4 percent, you would double your interest to about $2,600. This is a large increase in percentage terms, as it is a 100 percent increase, but on an absolute basis, it is only $1,300 more. With a mortgage, the change on an absolute basis is far more significant. If you have a $300,000 mortgage for thirty years at an interest rate of 2 percent, you would pay about $100,000 in interest. If you doubled the interest rate to 4 percent, you would, as with a car loan, double your total interest, to just over

$215,000. However, this time, you increased the total interest by $115,000 instead of $1,300. This is why getting your credit in order *before* getting a mortgage is so important—it can literally save, or cost, you hundreds of thousands of dollars.

Credit scores are slow moving but can also be volatile—it's an interesting dynamic. It is not uncommon for credit scores to vary wildly from month to month without anything substantial changing in your credit report, yet when you try to improve your score, it can take months to see any improvement. Since credit scores can be slow moving and take time to build, or rebuild, it is important to begin focusing on improving your credit months in advance of when you need to obtain the mortgage.

One of the largest factors in determining your credit score is your payment history. Unfortunately, the past cannot be changed, and therefore if you have a poor payment history, there is nothing you can do about that now. However, if you know you would like to begin house hacking in one to two years, be hyperfocused on your payment history over that period to ensure you do not miss another payment. This won't eliminate the negative payment history you have incurred, but it will help lessen its significance when it's time for you to apply for a mortgage.

The next two high-impact items are credit use and derogatory marks. Similar to your payment history, the back history of your derogatory marks cannot be changed—it has already happened. However, you *can* resolve these items if they are outstanding, such as paying a past-due medical bill or collection account. By resolving these items, they will lessen in severity over time and will be viewed much more favorably by a potential lender. For your credit use, it is important to reduce this as much as possible before your mortgage application. By reducing this number, you will not only improve your credit score; you will also reduce your monthly debt payments, which reduces your DTI ratio.

The next three factors in your credit score are your credit age, total number of accounts, and your hard inquiries. If you are planning to apply for a mortgage in a short period, there is not much you can do to increase the average age of your credit, increase your total accounts, or reduce your hard inquiries. The average age of your credit and your number of hard inquiries change over time, with your age of credit increasing over time and your hard inquiries falling off your report over time, but you cannot force time forward. You could increase your total accounts, but that often comes at the detriment of your credit age and hard inquiries. Each new account you open to increase your total account number decreases your credit age and increases your hard inquiries—moving both metrics in the wrong direction. On the bright side, these three metrics are often considered low-to-medium impact.

CHAPTER 11

Finding and Managing Your Tenants

Everything you have learned and done to this point has prepared you for starting your real estate investing journey. Now it's time to actually get started. In this chapter, you will learn how to define your tenant criteria, how to find your tenants, how to manage your tenants professionally, how a systematized screening process can help you avoid discrimination lawsuits, how to build systems and processes, how to be a professional landlord, and how to manage a previous owner's tenants that remain in a property you acquire.

Defining Your Tenant Criteria

If you think back to the beginning of your property search, you'll remember that one of the first steps before you began searching was to actually define what you were looking for and where you were looking to buy. The same process applies to finding your tenants. Sure, you can always put some ads out there and follow the steps in the next section, Finding Your Tenants, without defining your tenant criteria first, but how will you know which applicants you would like to have as tenants? You would not know which ones meet your qualifications for a "good tenant," and you might even get yourself into legal trouble.

Even if you do not intend to, you could find yourself accidentally breaking discrimination laws by not defining your criteria. An applicant you turn down could feel that your decision was not fair and just. If they were upset enough, they could file a complaint for discrimination. As part of the complaint, the government agency handling the claim would probably ask you to provide documentation proving why you chose one tenant over another. Even if you did not discriminate, it would be hard to provide documentation proving so without a set list of criteria. Having your criteria memorized is not enough. You must have physical evidence that you have a predefined set of criteria. You could also unintentionally discriminate if you do not have a list of criteria to compare against each applicant, which is still illegal. Ignorance is not bliss to the government agency in this case.

ALERT

Federal fair housing laws can and likely will change over time. Be sure to review the current laws when you plan to screen your potential tenants. If you research the laws while you read this book but don't screen tenants for a year or two, be sure to revisit the current laws at that time.

Define your criteria up front. That way, you do not have to worry about not being prepared if you ever have claims of discrimination. If you received the request for documentation from a government agency, you would be able to provide your list of criteria that you screen every applicant with and explain why the tenant you chose was the best applicant based on that criteria, as opposed to the one you declined.

To define your criteria, make a list of all the items that are important to you when screening a potential tenant that are not against the federal fair housing laws. For example, one of the most common is an applicant's income, specifically their income in relation to the rent. Many landlords require that the applicant's income be equal to three times the monthly rent. If the rent of their property is $1,000 per month, they would require their applicant's gross income to be at least $3,000 per month. This $3,000 per month could come from one person applying alone or from two people each making $1,500 per month.

If you think back to financial institutions' underwriting process, you can take a page out of their book. One example would be using a DTI ratio. On average, most landlords are satisfied with the three-times-rent criteria, which states that applicants' total gross monthly income must be at least three times the monthly rent. However, if you are a bit more conservative, you may choose to look at a renter's DTI ratio. Looking at the DTI ratio of potential applicants could be beneficial because one's income is not the only financial factor that determines their ability to pay. As an example, assume the rent is $1,000 per month; one applicant makes $5,000 per month, and the second applicant makes $3,000 per month. Based only on income, the first applicant looks like a stronger candidate than the latter applicant. But what if the first candidate also has a $600 car payment, $500 per month in credit card bills, and $1,000 per month in student loans, while the second applicant has no debt—they own their car outright and have no credit card bills or student loans. On a gross income basis, the first applicant is stronger, but on a DTI basis, the second applicant would be.

To get an accurate picture of an applicant's debt payments, you need to pull their credit report(s), but you are required to have their permission before doing so. If you decline an applicant because of information in their credit report, you must also provide them with an adverse action letter explaining why you rejected them, giving the name and address of the credit agency you received the information from, and telling the applicant they have a right to obtain a free copy of their credit report by requesting it from the credit agency you used within sixty days.

Even if you do not use a DTI ratio when screening tenants, you still might want to pull an applicant's credit report to get their credit score and review their payment history. You can and should set guidelines for what conditions are acceptable to you. As an example, you may decide to only consider applicants with a credit score above 650 and who do not have more than three late payments on their credit report within the last twelve months. The conditions you choose are up to you, as long as you consistently apply those requirements to all applicants equally.

In addition to an applicant's credit score and payment history, their credit report will show any history of bankruptcies and can show evictions as well. You can use such details to determine if you want to rent to them. One landlord may require that their tenants have no bankruptcies and have never been evicted, whereas another might be okay with a bankruptcy as long as it was more than five years ago, as an example.

Background Check

Another commonly used report when screening applicants is a background check. An applicant's background check generally shows their past criminal history or the lack thereof. More extensive background checks can include identity verification, driving history, education information, and employment history. Most landlords who use a background check are looking for past criminal activity. As long as you act in accordance with federal and state laws, which is crucial with all applicant screening criteria, you can choose what details of an applicant's criminal history are acceptable to you.

Employment History

Employment history is another important detail that many landlords consider when screening tenants. Not only does a person's income matter; the length of time they have been employed and the industry they work in can come into play as well. An applicant who has bounced around from job to job or has not been with their current employer long has a higher risk of not paying rent than someone who has been with the same employer for a decade. Remember, your criteria must be concrete and applicable across all applicants, so it is not enough to simply say that you require your tenants to be at their job a "long time." This amount must be quantified, such as "Tenants must have been with their employer for at least one year."

Some landlords may also consider the industry or company that an applicant works in. An applicant working in a brand-new industry or a startup company might be seen as a higher risk than someone who works for a well-established company and industry. According to the Bureau of Labor Statistics, nearly 45 percent of all new businesses fail within the first five years, so landlords do not want to have to guess which startups will last and which will not in order to determine if their renter's job is secure. The current state of an industry is often considered as well. During the beginning of the COVID-19 pandemic, many landlords added a criterion to their list that they would not accept new tenants that were working in the hospitality industry, as that industry was hit very hard by the virus. If an applicant's industry is experiencing a lot of unemployment or expected lay-offs in the near future, a landlord may add to their criteria that they will not rent to anyone in that industry.

References

References are another form of screening criteria used by landlords. The type of references that are required can vary. Some landlords only require references from the applicant's current landlord, if they have one, while others may also require a reference from their employer and a character reference. The character reference usually comes from a friend or family member. Asking for references seems like a no-brainer—why *wouldn't* you want to know about this person based on others' experiences, especially their current landlord? It is usually fair to assume that the way someone has acted in the past is probably going to continue in the future. How an applicant treated their current landlord's property is a pretty good indication of how they are going to treat your property. It makes sense, then, to include this criterion as a part of your screening process, right? Maybe, but maybe not.

The issue of references may not be as black and white as it seems. Charlie Munger, one of the most successful investors and businessmen of all time, has said, "Show me the incentive and I will show you the outcome." What are a landlord's incentives? Well, it depends on the tenant. Assume the tenant has always paid rent on time, they have lived in their current property for years, there have been no complaints or issues, and they have kept the property in great condition. If you call their landlord for a reference, they might truthfully describe their experience with the tenant; on the other hand, they might not be fully truthful with you, or they might not give a reference at all. Thinking about what Charlie Munger has said, what is the landlord incentivized to say?

If the landlord gives the tenant a glowing reference, there is a high probability that the landlord will lose a good tenant. If the landlord gives the tenant a negative reference or declines to provide one, then the landlord will be able to keep their good tenant.

Let's look at another example. The tenant in question does not pay on time, they consistently have issues and break rules, and they have not taken care of the property. If you call the landlord for a reference on this tenant, what is the landlord's incentive? In this case, they may be thrilled at the idea of this tenant moving out. Instead of being upset that the tenant might be leaving, the landlord would be excited to have this problem tenant move out. The landlord might lie to you and say the tenant has been a model tenant, or they may not say anything at all.

References from friends and family might be as unreliable as those from landlords. If the applicant is currently living with friends or family, what are the friends and family incentivized to say? It is less likely that a friend or family member would lie about a good or bad tenant, as the tenant's relationship with them is different than with a landlord. But if the experience has not been great, it is possible that the friend or family member might try to get the tenant off the property to alleviate the situation.

ALERT

Employers also have an interesting incentive dynamic. Most employers are unlikely to say negative things about an applicant during a reference check. Even if the employee in question is not the best worker, employers are unlikely to interfere in their personal life.

There is still more to consider when checking references. What is the applicant's incentive? Most likely, it is to be accepted as a tenant at your property. Because of this incentive, it is highly unlikely that an applicant is going to provide negative references that might jeopardize them getting approved. If the applicant knows that Aunt Suzie is going to say negative things about her, but Cousin Joe would only have amazing things to say, who is the applicant going to list as a reference?

One last aspect of references to consider is your ability as a landlord to defend your classification of a reference. All of the previous screening criteria are hard to argue, as long as you apply them consistently. The items involve quantitative data with no ambiguity or judgment. If you set your maximum DTI ratio at 55 percent, and a prospective tenant has a DTI ratio of 60 percent, the answer is clear. However, with a reference, what is quantified as "good"? What is considered "good enough"? How do you consistently and fairly assess that across many applicants without allowing any bias? Assume you had to respond to a complaint about potential discrimination—how would you prove your judgment of the approved applicant's references versus the complainant's references? Certain situations would be clear, while others could be much less so.

FACT

When checking references for potential applicants, be sure to keep records of the conversation, including the date and time of the call, whom you spoke with, and detailed notes. This will provide the proper documentation for your own reference and any legal issues that may arise.

References are often considered a must-have when hiring for a job or screening a potential tenant, but as you just learned, references may not carry the weight that many hiring managers and landlords think they do. This is not to say you should never ask for references. They can be valuable and useful, but you may not want to apply the heaviest weight to the reference criteria when screening tenants. Rather than *the* deciding factor, consider references as a small piece of the much larger screening pie.

Create an Applicant Tracker

Once you have decided how you are going to screen your applicants and then defined your benchmarks for each criterion, you can create a document that will act as a rubric. You can design this any way you would like, but a common design is to list all of your criteria on the left side, with the applicant's name at the top. Then you can check off each item on your list to indicate whether an applicant passed the criteria. Once you are finished, you can see which applicants meet all or most of your criteria. Many investors create an applicant tracker in Excel or Google Sheets, but you can use pen and paper if you prefer. If you do not want to make one yourself, you can find a copy of an applicant tracker here: https://everythinghousehacking.com/applicant-tracker. Using an applicant tracker will not only help you keep track of and analyze each tenant's application; it will also serve as an organized document to refer to if your screening process is ever questioned.

It is a good practice to include a link to each of the applicant's documents in your applicant tracker. If you have a credit score requirement on the left side of your tracker, you can note in the applicant column whether or not they met the criteria and include a link to their credit report. The same can be done for background checks, the application itself, or any other documentation you require.

Organization is an important skill that will be beneficial to you as an investor. Each applicant will have anywhere from two or three pages of documents to over a dozen. If you have several applicants, you may have over fifty pages of paperwork when you include their application, credit report(s), background check, and other documentation you require to satisfy your criteria. If you do not have an organized structure to store all of these documents, it can quickly become messy.

One way to organize your application documents is to create a folder for each property on your computer or in a cloud storage program, such as Google Drive, then create a subfolder in the property folder for each applicant. From there, you can create subfolders for each criterion you have, such as a folder for credit reports and one for background checks. You can also use a structured file-naming system instead of the subfolders. An example of this system would be to name each file with the document name, underscore, property number, and applicant's last name: "Credit Report_1234 Leonard." Whichever file-naming convention you use, it should be consistent across all documentation to ensure things stay organized and make it easy to find each document, property, and applicant.

Finding Your Tenants

You know exactly what you are looking for and what you consider to be an acceptable tenant. Now it is time to actually find them. In Chapter 5, you learned all about building your real estate team. Your team is going to have an impact on how you approach finding tenants.

If you chose to forgo a property manager, which most house hackers do, it is your responsibility to find your tenants. This does not mean you have to do it alone. In addition to helping you find your property, a real estate agent should be able to help you find your tenants. Reach out to your agent and ask for their assistance. They might have a network of renters that they are helping to find a property that they can connect you with, or they can list your property for rent on the MLS. Your agent may also be willing to conduct the showings with potential tenants for you. Using a real estate agent in this tenant-finding capacity will often require a fee. In some cases, it is a commission based on the rental amount, such as 50 percent of the first month's rent, or it can be a flat fee.

ESSENTIAL

Before you commit to using your agent to find tenants, be sure you understand their cost structure. If they offer to help you for free, it is a good practice to compensate them with an amount you think is fair. Providing you with favors is only going to last so long, but if you compensate them sufficiently, they'll be more likely to help you indefinitely going forward.

It is possible to find tenants on your own without your agent. The MLS can be a great source of leads for potential tenants, so if you still want to list your property on the MLS but do not want to use an agent for the rest, you can pay an MLS listing fee to an agent with no other requirements from them, or you can sign up for an online platform that has a one-time fee for listing your property on the MLS. One of the benefits of the MLS listing is that it automatically gets picked up by all of the third-party sites, such as Zillow, Redfin, and others, which receive the majority of the traffic and leads. Many of these platforms, however, allow you to list your rentals directly on their site without going through the MLS. Unless your property management software does this for you, you will have to create listings separately yourself on each platform, but it is possible without the MLS.

Outside of the traditional channels for tenant acquisition, you can also use word of mouth, social media platforms, and paid marketing. Simply mentioning to your friends and family who live in the area where you are looking could help find a tenant. Someone's cousin or friend may have just mentioned to them that they were looking for a new place to live. You can also post on your social media accounts that you are looking for someone to rent your property. A friend or follower you have not spoken with in years may see your post and be a great tenant for you.

ALERT

Regardless of how you find your tenants, be sure to do your due diligence and screen everyone against your criteria. It is rarely a good practice to accept a tenant solely because they are a friend, a family member, or a friend of a friend.

You can also use other areas of social media platforms, such as Facebook Marketplace and Facebook Groups. There is an entire category on Facebook Marketplace to list your property for rent. Craigslist used to be one of the most popular sites to list rental units, but it has been overtaken in recent years by Facebook Marketplace. In addition to the marketplace, you can look at different Facebook Groups for specific towns and cities. If your town or city has a Facebook Group, you may be able to find a tenant by posting about your opening in that group.

Google Ads and Facebook Ads are paid marketing strategies that could help you find tenants. This is the least common of the options listed for individual investors. But if you are operating in a very competitive market or are struggling to find tenants with the other strategies, Google Ads and Facebook Ads using targeted keywords related to rental availability in your area *could* bring you applicants.

You can also check with local universities, hospitals, businesses, or real estate offices to see if they have any programs for students or faculty looking for housing. Schools and universities sometimes "partner" with landlords to provide students with housing if/when the school can't. In addition, some businesses and hospitals have to occasionally help their staff find housing. If all else fails, use your creativity. There are a number of ways you can find tenants—do not be afraid of testing your own new strategies if necessary.

Professional Tenant Management

One of the best things you can do during your real estate investing journey is to be professional. That does not mean you have to own hundreds of units or manage large apartment buildings. It means running your business like a business, no matter the size. This may seem obvious, but you would be surprised how many real estate investors treat their business like a hobby instead of a business. If you treat it like a hobby, you will struggle to scale, have loads of headaches like subpar quality tenants, labor intensive instead of passive, trouble at tax time, messy bookkeeping, and so on, and probably will not make much profit.

Even if you are house hacking a single-family property and renting by the room, start treating it like a business now. You have probably heard at some point in your life that habits are hard to break. Well, if you start out on the right foot and build the right habits from the beginning, you will not have to worry about breaking your bad habits later on.

Just by doing what you have learned in this chapter about screening tenants—having defined criteria, a rubric, and an organized system—you are many steps ahead of the "mom-and-pop" real estate investors. While that is a great start, that is really just the first step. You must maintain the same approach throughout all aspects of your real estate business.

The Lease

After you have gone through the screening process and found your tenant, you must manage them professionally. This starts with having a formal lease. You can use one of the many free or premium templates available on the Internet, you can ask your real estate agent for the legal lease form that many state-specific real estate associations have, or you can ask an attorney to draft a lease for you. Whichever route you choose, ensure the lease covers the specifics of your situation. If your tenant is responsible for mowing the lawn or taking care of certain utilities, for example, be sure to include those items in your lease.

Your lease should also include which forms of payment you accept for rent and how those rent payments need to be made. A common mistake of unprofessional landlords is to accept rent in cash and to pick it up monthly from tenants. This is especially common for house hackers because of how convenient it is. If you are a landlord who lives thirty minutes from your rental properties, it is harder to collect cash each month (surprisingly, people still do it!), but if you are a house hacker who lives right next door, it is much more convenient. Convenience does not mean it is the right approach.

Instead, you should set up a system to collect payments electronically. There are numerous property management software programs to choose from (you can find a list of recommended resources here: https://everythinghousehacking.com/recommended-resources). Quite a few of them are free to landlords and charge the tenants a small fee for processing their rent. These platforms allow tenants to set up automatic payments and automatic late fees, and some even enable tenants to pay via credit card, which can increase the probability of you receiving payment. Each month, as rent is received, the money is deposited directly into the bank account you have linked to the software on your end.

Property Management Software

Property management software is the cornerstone of managing your properties professionally. At first, especially with a house hack, it may seem like overkill, but it is a very valuable tool for you to scale. As you buy more house hacks, or even traditional rental properties, you can simply add your new properties and tenants to your already existing system.

Property management software not only allows you to collect rent; it also provides a place for tenants to submit maintenance requests, for you to communicate with your tenants, and even a way to store your documentation. Rather than tenants texting you at all hours of the night every time there is an issue with their unit, they can simply be directed to submit a maintenance request. You can then forward the request to the party who will resolve it. For example, if there is an issue with the toilet, you can forward the maintenance request to the plumber that you have already built a relationship with (see Chapter 5). Now, instead of dealing with the dreaded "tenants, taxes, and toilets," you have built a system that is semi-passive and takes very little work on your end.

ALERT

Most real estate investors get into the business as a way to obtain financial freedom through generating passive income. If you do not build the necessary systems and processes, you are buying yourself a job instead of a passive, or semi-passive, income stream. Buying another job will not get you to financial freedom.

Whether you are communicating about a maintenance request or a non-maintenance issue, property management software allows you to have those conversations within its platform. You do not have the cell phone number for the chief executive officer at Apple, do you? The same goes for your tenants. Not only is it a pain when your tenants text you; it is also unprofessional and not how business should be conducted. Text messages should be reserved for emergency use only.

Earlier in the chapter, you learned about having an organized system for storing applicants' documentation. That system is still likely necessary for all of the applicant's documentation, but you can store the documents of the applicant that you approved and became your tenant *in* the property management software. You can even make certain documents available to your tenants, such as the leases and your policies, so they can easily access them.

Managing a Previous Owner's Tenants

Not every real estate transaction you participate in will have a clean transition with tenants. You may purchase a vacant property, but it is also possible that you will acquire a property with existing tenants. Every investor has their own opinion on whether or not they want tenants in the property at the time of acquiring it. Some want immediate income and do not want to deal with finding tenants, while others do not want to rely on a previous owner's tenant screening. You can decide which you prefer, but regardless of your preference, let's look at how to manage tenants you acquire with a property.

A common issue house hackers face is trying to buy a property that is already full of tenants. In a traditional home purchase, the seller and owner of the property moves out when the sale is complete, and the buyer moves in. However, it is quite common when buying a property to house hack that the property is owned as a true investment property by another investor, in which case they would not be residing in the property. Using a duplex as an example, another investor may own this property and have it rented to two separate tenants. If you are trying to acquire this property, it would be fine as a traditional investment property; you would simply acquire the two tenants as well. However, because you are using an owner-occupied mortgage product and plan to live in one of the units, this situation would not work. You would have to be able to occupy the property within the time frame described in your loan documents. A solution to this is if the tenants are on month-to-month leases, the current owner could ask one of the tenants to vacate upon or before the sale of the property. If the tenants are on yearlong leases or do not want to leave, you would not be able to move forward with acquiring that property to house hack.

Assuming the owner can get one of the units vacant, or that there is already an open unit for you to move into after you acquire it, the next focus is on managing the existing tenants. First, you should be sure to acquire all relevant documentation from the current owner, such as leases, late payment notices, and security deposits. These documents are often transferred at closing. Once all documentation has been received, you should review it in detail to ensure you understand all aspects of it. In most cases, the lease from the previous owner is still valid when you acquire the property, unless you get the tenant to void the previous lease and sign a new one, so it is important to understand what rules and guidelines you are now upholding. You will also want to understand when the lease started, when it ends, and how payments are made.

Once you understand the full picture, there are two situations you could face. The first is that the lease is relatively new or at least won't be expiring in the near future. In this case, there is little you can do to change the terms of the lease, but you can still implement all the professional tenant management strategies you learned in this chapter, such as getting the tenant set up in your property management software and collecting rent payments electronically.

The second situation is when the lease is up within the next month or two. In this case, you will want to start planning your next steps because you will have much more flexibility once the existing lease is up. Your first decision is whether or not you will ask the tenant to vacate the property. If you do ask the tenant to vacate, be sure to fully understand and follow all the legal requirements around this process. Once the tenant has vacated, you will need to complete any necessary repairs or renovations to get the unit rent-ready, and then you are free to begin the screening process you learned in this chapter.

If you will not be asking the tenant to vacate and you are happy with the lease that was in place, you can simply provide the tenant with a copy of the same lease and just update the dates. If you are not completely satisfied with the lease, or you do not have a blank copy of the existing lease, you can follow the steps you learned for getting a lease document. However, be careful how you approach the rental amount. Depending on the previous owner's level of professionalism and how long the tenant was in the property, the tenant's rental rate may not be accurate—if anything, it will be too low.

When the rental rate is too low, it is worth considering the feasibility of the situation. Assume rent is currently $1,000 per month, but based on your research, the market rate is actually $1,500 per month. This might seem extreme, but you would be surprised how often this actually happens, especially with unprofessional landlords. In most cases like this, it isn't reasonable to expect the tenants to be able to afford a $500 per month increase with no notice. Therefore, you must consider the second-order consequences of your next move; it is not a simple decision.

As a professional landlord, you want to consider all of the possible scenarios and make the best-informed decision you can. If you increase rent to the market rate, which is fair, the tenant may not be able to pay it. They may move out, or they may cause a problem by not paying *and* not leaving. If they do leave, you have to consider the amount of work and its associated cost to get the unit rent-ready, as well as the payback period.

ESSENTIAL

Unit turnover is one of the largest drains on a real estate investor's profitability. The rehab amount may not seem like a lot on its own, but if you consider how long it will take to earn that money back from the $500 per month increase you would receive, you may find it isn't worth it.

One of your other options is to keep rent the same. Maybe you want to keep the tenants and your numbers make sense at the current rent, or perhaps you have decided that the rehab needed to get the unit rent-ready isn't worth it at this time. Your last option is to increase the rent amount, but by less than the amount needed to get to the market rate. In hopes of keeping the tenants that are in place and avoiding a rehab, you may choose to increase rent by $100 or $200, instead of $500. The tenants won't like a rent increase, but if you keep the amount reasonable and affordable for them, they are unlikely to go through the hassle of moving.

Almost as important as the amount that you choose to increase rent is how you present the tenants with the increase. If you simply write up a new lease and drop it in their mailbox or email the document without any context, they probably won't be very happy. Instead, be professional and conduct the transaction in a businesslike manner. You do not necessarily owe them an explanation, but it can help ease the situation and maintain the relationship to show them your reasoning. You have already done the research you learned in Chapter 8 to determine the market rate, so provide them with your findings. Give them the reports and data that support the increased rate. Show them that the market rate, what you could have raised the rent to, is higher than what you actually raised it to.

CHAPTER 12

Your Property's Financials

You may not be an accountant or love bookkeeping, but accurate financial records play a vital role in your real estate business. In this chapter, you will learn why bookkeeping is important, how to set up a bookkeeping system, what to look for in a bookkeeping tool or software, how house hacking impacts your taxes, and what virtual assistants are, why they are important for your real estate investing journey, and how to find one.

The Importance of Bookkeeping

In Chapter 11, you learned about what it means to be a professional and how to operate as one. In this chapter, you are going to learn about another aspect of being a professional and treating your rental properties as a business—bookkeeping. It is certainly not glamorous, nor is it the part of real estate investing people look forward to most, but it is important.

A quick Internet search would show you many examples of mom-and-pop investors who *still* do their record-keeping with pen and paper. You might be surprised, given the resources that are available today, but many investors are part of the generation that did not have those options. Technological advancements have begun to make their way into real estate, but historically, there has not been much innovation in the industry. Using these tools, specifically for your bookkeeping, will not only help you treat your rentals like a business and be a professional; they will also save you time and help you make more money.

ALERT

As you grow as a real estate investor, you will come across situations where you are thankful for mom-and-pop and unprofessional owners. You should not operate as one yourself, but you can often find great opportunities to buy deals from them.

On the hit TV show *Shark Tank*, Kevin "Mr. Wonderful" O'Leary frequently interrogates the entrepreneurs about knowing their numbers. He does not do this just to antagonize them; there is a valid business reason behind it. How can you make decisions about your business if you do not know your numbers? In an entrepreneurial sense, if you are paying $10 to acquire a customer through paid marketing channels and only have a customer lifetime value of $8, you are losing $2 on every customer, on average. Without this information, you may continue to pour money into this marketing channel because you can see your top line revenue going up, which makes you assume it is doing well, but you do not see that you are actually burning cash.

A similar situation can occur with house hacking. In Chapter 8, you learned how to analyze a house hack deal, and you rightfully made a lot of assumptions when completing your analysis. How will you know if those assumptions are accurate if you do not consistently keep accurate books? What if, based on your analysis, you expected your contribution to the monthly mortgage to be $250 per month, when in reality it is actually $600? By keeping accurate books, you can track your information very quickly, which will allow you to make decisions to prevent problems. You can see where your analysis went wrong so you can improve your assumptions for future deal analyses, and it could highlight something that you are over-paying for. If you understand your numbers, you can make rational business decisions based on data, not emotions, and that is only possible if you have accurate bookkeeping.

When the first tax season comes around after you have started invest ing in real estate, you will be very thankful you kept detailed, organized records—especially with house hacking. One of the four pillars of real estate investing is tax benefits, but in order to take advantage of those, you will need the necessary supporting documentation. If you keep track throughout the year, it can be an easy process come tax time, but if you do not, it will be a time-consuming and frustrating process, and you may even miss some of the tax benefits available to you.

FACT

The four pillars of real estate are cash flow, appreciation, tax benefits, and equity paydown. They are the main benefits that make real estate investing as a whole such an effective strategy—one that not many other strategies can match.

If you have invested your time and energy into reading this book, learning about house hacking, and actually applying what you have learned, you probably will not stop at house hacking one property. You may be on your way to multiple house hacks or buying rental properties. Buying more properties, whether they are house hacks or traditional rental properties, before you have the right systems and processes in place is only going to make it more difficult to implement them in the future. Develop your bookkeeping system when you have just one house hack, when it is relatively simple, then you can apply that same system over and over to multiple properties. Also, similar to your taxes, having your bookkeeping organized will make providing the required documentation to your future lender much easier and less time-consuming. Having your bookkeeping in order makes scaling up much easier.

You may absolutely dread bookkeeping, as many people do. If so, you will be happy to learn that you do not have to do it forever. You may not even have to do it at all. How? Outsourcing.

Outsourcing

The most straightforward way to avoid bookkeeping is to outsource it to an accounting or bookkeeping firm. However, this is also the most expensive option and probably overkill for a single house hack. Even as you scale, these firms may be too expensive for a relatively small portfolio. Instead, you can hire a virtual assistant for a much lower cost. This approach is a bit more labor-intensive in the short run, but the cost savings and flexibility are often worth it. You *can* hire a virtual assistant and ask them to build your bookkeeping system for you, but it is better to build it yourself so that you fully understand it, then you can hand it off to a virtual assistant in the future. Also, having experience in a specific role or with a certain task before hiring it out gives you a better understanding of what you need in a candidate for that position. Later in this chapter, you will learn exactly how to use a virtual assistant for your bookkeeping needs, but for now, just understand that you do not have to be stuck with the bookkeeping duties forever if you don't want to be.

Tools and Software for Real Estate Bookkeeping

You have learned the importance of consistent, accurate bookkeeping, and now you are ready to find the right tools or software—assuming you do not want to stick with pen and paper. The tools and software mentioned in this chapter may change over time. Some may be discontinued, and it is almost guaranteed that more will become available. If these tools and software are available to you at the time you need them for bookkeeping, they are worth considering (you can find an up-to-date list of the best tools and platforms here: https://everythinghousehacking.com/recommended-resources). But if they are not available, or you simply do not like them, you can apply the criteria you learn here to your search for the right tools.

> **ESSENTIAL**
>
> As you near the end of this book, think about a common theme—taking the principles, strategies, or criteria described throughout this book and applying them to your specific situation. If nothing else, one of the biggest takeaways from this book is learning how to learn, then applying those learnings to your own life.

You may not need to look any further than the property management software you set up during your screening process for a bookkeeping tool or software. Some property management platforms also provide bookkeeping features in addition to their tenant screening and management features. If you are happy with the platform you found, it can be quite convenient to keep all, or as many as possible, investing-related tasks in one platform. Since your tenants will be paying you through the property management software, it is easy to simply record those payments automatically in your accounting records when they are received. Even maintenance requests that your tenants submit through that platform can be tied to expenses in your accounting records.

If your property management software does not offer accounting features or if you are not completely happy with the product, you can use another platform specifically for bookkeeping. There are accounting and bookkeeping platforms that are focused on real estate investors. One of the leading platforms designed specifically for real estate investors is Stessa. The major benefit of real estate–specific software is that it includes features that are geared toward investors. For example, the income statement for a rental property is slightly different than that of a traditional business. Having an income statement tailored to your industry helps you look at the right metrics related to your business, and it makes your tax professional's job easier.

That does not mean that you shouldn't use a general accounting software. QuickBooks has been a longtime powerhouse of the accounting software industry. Although it is not specifically made for real estate investing, many investors use it with great success. A similar platform to QuickBooks that may be even better for a house hacker is Wave. QuickBooks is not very expensive, but it does have a cost. At this time, Wave is completely free for bookkeeping, which fits well into a house hacker's model.

Maybe you are more of a do-it-yourself kind of person who enjoys playing in Excel. It can be a bit more labor-intensive and time-consuming, but this software can be a great option because of its flexibility. With a prebuilt software tool, you are limited to what the platform offers. However, with Excel or Google Sheets, the possibilities and flexibility are nearly endless. You can use templates (you can find these at https://everythinghousehacking.com/recommended-resources) and customize them to fit your needs, or you can start entirely from scratch. There are also many virtual assistants available that are already familiar with how to use Excel and Google Sheets. You can certainly train them to use whichever software tool you prefer, but if you use Excel or Google Sheets, there may be less of a learning curve for your virtual assistant.

ALERT

If you choose to create your own bookkeeping system in Google Sheets or Excel, be sure to build in a process for storing receipts. A common way to do this is to pair your file with a cloud storage program, such as Google Drive. Simply save the receipts in the cloud storage program and insert a link to each receipt in the bookkeeping file you created next to the transaction.

When searching for the right software tool for your bookkeeping, use these criteria: basic features, cost, advanced or specific features, ease of access and cross-platform availability, and whether or not it is scalable. First, start by considering the bare-minimum features you need for your bookkeeping and immediately eliminate any tools that do not have those features. With house hacking, you are probably trying to be wise with your money and looking to reduce your living cost. Using expensive software just to do your bookkeeping for one or a few rental units is counterproductive. There are many options available, such as Wave and Google Sheets, that are free or affordably priced.

Once you have moved past the bare-minimum features required, you may want specific or advanced features. Maybe you need to be able to export your data to Excel or a PDF. Maybe you want a customizable dashboard with key performance indicators. Create a list of every feature you consider valuable versus which ones are deal breakers. Remove any products from your search that do not have your deal-breaking features.

FACT

A famous quote often attributed to Benjamin Franklin is "If you fail to plan, you are planning to fail." This sentiment applies to all of your house hacking processes, even your bookkeeping. Rather than picking the first software you find, consider what is important to you and find the best fit for your long-term plans and goals, not just what seems best in the moment.

With the technology and tools available today, an important consideration is how easily you can access your bookkeeping software and if you can use it across multiple platforms. If you are considering software that only works on PCs and you have a Mac, or vice versa, that software will not work for you. You may want to be able to access the software across multiple platforms and devices, such as your computer, phone, and tablet. If the bookkeeping software only works on your computer, that may be an issue for you.

Lastly, you will want to consider how the bookkeeping software scales. Right now, you may only own one rental unit as part of your duplex house hack. But what about in a year or two, when you buy another house hack and keep your current one as a rental? What if you buy another three to seven rental properties over the next few years? It is in your best interest to consider your future plans when you are just starting out. You will want to know if the software can handle bookkeeping and reporting for more than one property in a way that fits your needs. Also, if you pick a bookkeeping software with your future plans and scalability in mind, you will not have to train your virtual assistant to use it again, nor will you have to learn a new software yourself. Your virtual assistant can just replicate what they are currently doing for your house hack process with any future rentals, saving you time and money.

House Hacking Taxes

The tax code in the United States is extremely complex and dense. There are hundreds of thousands of individuals who dedicate their entire careers to studying this material, as well as hundreds of large firms that provide tax-related services. There are numerous books written about various tax topics, and everyone's situation is different. Because this book is not allowed to legally give tax advice, only the most important, basic tax items related to house hacking will be covered, but you are encouraged to get more detailed and individual-specific advice from a qualified tax professional.

To summarize the extremely complex and dense US tax code as simply as possible, most citizens are required to pay a certain amount each year (the amount is based on their income and life situation) to the Internal Revenue Service (IRS). This is known as an annual tax bill and is typically paid in installments throughout the year via a paycheck. At the end of the year, if the person paid more in taxes than their total tax bill amount, the difference is returned to them in the form of a tax refund. There are many nuances to this process, and different tax credits and initiatives impact one's annual tax bill differently, but in a very simplified manner, this is how an individual's taxes are determined.

Tax Deductions

A tax write-off is an expense you paid that you are allowed to deduct from your income on your taxes to lower your tax bill. In theory, the more tax deductions you have, the more your annual tax bill is reduced, and, therefore, the less you have to pay, or the more you get in the form of a refund. When you are a traditional homeowner, there are usually very few expenses related to your home that you can write off. However, when you house hack, the number of expenses you can write off increases significantly.

When you are house hacking, your rental units are technically considered a business, even without having a registered legal entity. Filling out a Schedule C form in your tax return allows you to deduct expenses related to that business activity. The deductions have to be proportional to the amount of the property used for a rental. Let's look at an example of a duplex house hack to understand which items are tax deductible and how the proportionality works.

> **ALERT**
>
> There is a common misconception in the real estate industry, especially for newer investors, that an LLC (limited liability company) is required to start investing in real estate or is needed to receive tax deductions. Having an LLC to invest may be the right option for you, but it is not required. Talk with your tax professional and an attorney to determine what is right, and necessary, for you.

The two units in a duplex are not necessarily the same size or layout, but they are usually quite similar, if not identical. Therefore, let's assume you have a townhouse-style duplex with side-by-side units. The total square footage of livable space in the building is 2,400, which is split evenly between the two units—1,200 in each unit. This breakdown of livable square footage allocation is important when you are deducting your expenses proportionally. Generally speaking, since 50 percent of the square footage of this building is used as a rental property, you can write off 50 percent of tax-deductible expenses.

Tax-deductible expenses can apply to many different areas. One of the most common is landscaping and/or landscaping equipment. If you live in an area where it snows, half of your cost for snow removal should be tax deductible, since half of it is for your rental unit. Similarly, if you hire a landscaping company rather than doing it yourself, you should be able to deduct half of that cost. If you do your landscaping yourself, you may be able to deduct half of your cost of purchasing a lawn mower, snowblower, weed trimmer, or other equipment that is required to maintain the property. This same approach can be extrapolated across many, many areas that relate to the property. If it is required for the property or rental unit, it may be tax deductible.

ESSENTIAL

While being able to write off 50 percent of an expense is a great benefit of house hacking, it can get even better. Instead of a duplex, imagine you purchased a four-plex and lived in one of the units. You may now be able to deduct 75 percent of the expense. Depending on the square footage of the unit you're living in, if it's much less than the other units, you may be able to deduct even more!

Depreciation

Another major tax benefit of house hacking is depreciation. Depreciation is a non-cash, accounting expense that you can often deduct from your rental income when house hacking. The IRS allows investors to write off depreciation as a way to account for the wear and tear a property receives. The logic behind this tax code is that a property can only be used for so many years before it needs to be renovated or becomes inhabitable. The IRS has determined how long a property is supposed to remain in habitable condition, so you are allowed to write off a portion of the property's value each year over that period.

The non-cash portion of the depreciation definition is important because it means that you are not outlaying or losing any of the cash in your pocket. Rather, it is an accounting number that shows on your financial statements.

You can reduce your income, and therefore your annual tax bill, without actually having to spend any money. Be sure to connect with a qualified real estate–specific tax professional to discuss the details of your situation, what you can deduct, and how depreciation may work with your property.

> **FACT**
>
> As of this writing, the IRS requires real estate investors to use a "useful life" (the period during which an asset provides benefits) of twenty-seven and a half years when calculating depreciation on a residential rental property, such as a house hack.

Two-Out-of-Five-Year Rule

The two-out-of-five-year rule is a bit more well known and easier to understand than the 1031 exchange that you will learn about next. According to the IRS, the two-out-of-five-year rule says that if you have lived in a property for a minimum of two years in the past five years before the sale of the property, you can exclude up to $250,000 of your gains for individuals, and up to $500,000 for a joint return. The good news is that you do not have to live in the property at the time of the sale; you just have to have lived there for two of the last five years. A great way to use this strategy is to buy a house hack and live there for two years while you save for the down payment for your next house hack. Then, once you have enough money saved, buy your second house hack and move there, keep the first house hack as a traditional rental, and then sell it in just under three years from the date you moved out. If you set this up properly, you could build a ladder of these transactions by doing this for one house hack, then another, then another, and so on.

1031 Exchange

A 1031 exchange, which gets its name from Section 1031 in the US Internal Revenue Code, allows you to defer paying the amount owed on your capital gains from the sale of an investment property if those funds are reinvested into an asset of like kind within the specified time frame. For example, you may be able to use a 1031 exchange to defer the capital gains taxes you owe on an investment property that you bought for $100,000 that is now worth $500,000, if you use the proceeds from the sale of the property to buy another investment property that is similar to the one you just sold. A 1031 exchange is very complex and involves a lot of specific rules that need to be followed in order to do it properly and legally. The important takeaway is to understand that this *may* be an option for your house hack, and it should be noted as something to discuss with your tax professional and/or a 1031 exchange advisor.

Hiring a Professional

It can be very easy to fall down a black hole of tax strategy and all its intricacies. Rather than spending your time on becoming an expert, try to understand the basics and hire out the specifics to a professional. This professional will not only handle the specific tax code items that apply to your situation; they should also be able to guide you on what information you need to track throughout the year. It is important to note that a tax professional is not necessarily your bookkeeper. If you choose to outsource your bookkeeping to an accounting or bookkeeping firm, then a tax professional could also be your bookkeeper, but if you have decided to do it yourself or use a virtual assistant, the tax professional is separate. You or your virtual assistant will handle your day-to-day accounting and bookkeeping, and your tax professional will take that information and complete your tax filings. While the two are separate and different, they are also related. Your tax professional can help guide you as you set up your bookkeeping system and processes to ensure you are recording the necessary information and not wasting your time on items that do not matter.

Using a Virtual Assistant

At the beginning of this chapter, your interest was piqued by the idea of not having to do your bookkeeping yourself. The recommended way to remove yourself from the bookkeeping work is to hire a virtual assistant. But what is a virtual assistant?

The definition of a virtual assistant is revealed in its name—it is an assistant who completes work for you virtually, or remotely. The concept of an assistant is a familiar one; many high-level managers at corporations employ assistants who help them with various administrative tasks. This model is not as accessible to small-time entrepreneurs, however, because assistants are typically hired as employees, which means a full salary with benefits and requiring space in a physical location like an office environment.

Virtual assistants were created to solve these problems. They are usually not considered employees, meaning no benefits, and they do not need office space. Many virtual assistants work for several clients at the same time, so they may not require a 9-to-5 job situation. This model of virtual assistants combined with technological improvements allows professionals in all fields to hire people from anywhere in the world.

> **ESSENTIAL**
>
> The virtual assistant model uses a type of worker that has become increasingly popular over the past decade—the freelancer. A freelancer is typically paid on a per-job or per-task basis and is not tied to any one employer.

Understanding what virtual assistants are, how they work, and the opportunities available to you is important for you as a real estate investor and entrepreneur. Your virtual assistant is not limited to only bookkeeping tasks. They certainly can take that work off your plate, but that is just the beginning. The only limitation to what your virtual assistant can do for you is your own comfort level. Much of what you have learned throughout this book about house hacking can and should be applied to your future real estate investing endeavors—virtual assistants included. Once you know how to find talented, affordable virtual assistants, you can leverage this opportunity time and time again as you scale your portfolio.

There are many ways to find and hire a virtual assistant—new platforms are popping up every day. You will not benefit from the more affordable labor aspect mentioned previously, but you do not have to find someone via an online platform—you could find someone local to you, if you prefer.

One of the best online platforms is Upwork. This strategy is so good, in fact, there have been multiple bestselling books written about finding and hiring virtual assistants. The Upwork platform is easy to use, has a great pool of candidates, allows you to track the virtual assistant's screen to ensure they are doing the work they were assigned, and it's affordable and quick to set up.

One of the great things about these third-party platforms is that there are a ton of available freelancers. However, one of the downsides is also that there are a ton of freelancers on the platform. It is great that there are a lot of people to choose from, but it can often be overwhelming or make it difficult to filter through the quantity to find quality talent that you can rely on.

The following suggestions should help you filter out the noise, sift through the available virtual assistants, and find quality talent on Upwork. Once you are ready to start looking for your virtual assistant, the first step is to create an account. Then you will have two options: (1) post a job or (2) use the search bar to look for freelancers. Generally, it is best to start by posting a job with all the details of what you are looking for. After the job is live on the platform, you will probably get a lot of applicants, most of which will not meet your criteria. The process for screening virtual assistant applicants is quite similar to the tenant screening process you learned in Chapter 11; it just uses different criteria and is a bit easier.

ALERT

You can simply decline the applicant responses that do not meet your criteria. You can leave an explanation as to why you declined them, but it is not required. Then you will have a short list of applicants that do meet, or exceed, your criteria.

Unless you are completely satisfied with the candidates who responded to your post, you should also use the search bar to look for virtual assistants yourself. Once you have entered a search for "virtual assistant," it is very important to use the filtering options to narrow the results to only those that meet your criteria.

You may be wondering, "What are these 'criteria'?" Like when screening tenants, your virtual assistant screening criteria are the items and qualities that are must-haves for the position. The criteria you choose are entirely up to you, but following are some suggestions for criteria that have been successfully used by many real estate investors and entrepreneurs. Use what you wish, discard what you don't, and add what you'd like.

The first criterion is to search for "freelancers" under talent type. This will remove any agencies from your search criteria. Agencies tend to be a bit more expensive than individuals and harder to work with. The next criterion is to set the hourly rate at $10 and below. Of course, you can pay more than this, but you can often find a high-quality virtual assistant in this pay range.

The third criterion is to set the job success option to 90 percent and up. Ideally, you are only looking at candidates with a 99 percent or higher job success rate, but the platform does not allow you to filter for anything above 90 percent. Start with the 90 percent success rate, then look for only those with 99 percent or higher. You are almost certainly going to filter out quality talent that could do a great job for you. The reality is that some of those with a success rate of less than 99 percent could have just been unlucky by working for someone who is impossible to please. Due to the vast amount of options available, you can use strict filtering guidelines and still have a large enough candidate pool. This will ideally leave you with only the best of the best.

The next two criteria are finding candidates who have earned over $100 and billed more than one hundred hours within the last six months. Both of these criteria are set to serve the same purpose—finding only those candidates who are active and have a verifiable track record of working as a freelancer. You do not want your pool of candidates to be filled with profiles of freelancers who are no longer active on the platform, nor do you want candidates whose success rate is artificially high due to a small sample size from a lack of work history.

The last criterion to set is an English level of "fluent." While there are certainly talented candidates who are not fluent in English, working with anyone on a consistent basis is significantly easier if you speak the same language. The English criterion becomes even more important if you eventually hire a virtual assistant for work other than just bookkeeping, such as client- or tenant-facing work.

Some of the terminology used to describe these criteria is specific to the Upwork platform (you can find a video walk-through showing exactly how to use Upwork with these criteria to find a virtual assistant here: https://everythinghousehacking.com/upwork-virtual-assistants). However, you can apply the idea of the criteria to any platform or resource you use to find a virtual assistant. In a more general sense, the criteria were set to find a person in an area of the world where labor is more affordable, who is easy to communicate with, who has a verifiable track record of providing quality work, and who has been recently active. Following these steps will give you all the necessary information to find a qualified virtual assistant for your team in just a few hours.

Bookkeeping and managing your property's financials are really just the tip of the iceberg for what your virtual assistant can do for your business. A qualified virtual assistant can handle a significant portion of your real estate investing tasks if you have built the proper systems. Remember setting up your property management software to handle maintenance requests? There is no need for you to forward those messages to the appropriate people. Instead, you can have the nonemergency maintenance requests go directly to your trained virtual assistant, who has your list of team members, and they can simply forward the email with the required work to the right person. If it is a task that you are comfortable with someone else doing and you can teach someone how to do it, your virtual assistant can take it off your plate.

CHAPTER 13

Building On Your Experience

You did it! You bought your first house hack, and now you are ready to retire and ride off into the sunset. Not quite—house hacking is just the beginning. Now it is time to take what you have learned and apply it to scaling your real estate portfolio. In this chapter, you will learn the ways house hacking strategies and processes can and should be applied to other disciplines of real estate investing, why house hacking has a bigger impact on your finances than just the numbers, exit strategies, how to pivot your investing approach, and how to become a better real estate investor through self-reflection.

How House Hacking Relates to Other Real Estate Strategies

The most commonly mentioned benefit of house hacking is the financial one—house hacking can reduce or eliminate your largest expense. That certainly is one of the best benefits of house hacking and why more people should use the strategy. However, arguably more important is the experience that you gain by house hacking, and what that experience enables you to do.

If you save $1,000 per month by house hacking, that is fantastic and is a huge win over traditional homeownership. But using the experience you gain while house hacking could earn you multiple thousands, say, $5,000 as an example, per month in the future. Instead of only house hacking and saving money on your housing costs, you can use your house hacking experience to buy multiple rental properties that could provide even more income in total than house hacking.

Some may argue, "Why house hack then?" There are three main reasons. Not everyone has the funds available to purchase a rental right away, some people are not comfortable with starting with a rental property, and you can combine the two strategies of house hacking and traditional rentals to be even more powerful. Buying a rental property requires a 20–30 percent down payment plus closing costs, so it can cost tens of thousands of dollars, if not hundreds of thousands, depending on the purchase price. Someone just starting out with investing probably does not have the funds to cover the down payment. House hacking can help solve this problem by allowing people to save money on a monthly basis, which can then be put toward the down payment and closing costs on a rental property. As an example, a house hacker who saves $1,000 per month by house hacking can put that money aside and have $12,000 to buy their first rental property in just twelve months. Depending on where you are buying a property, you may not be able to purchase a large or multiunit property with $12,000, but if you can use a seller credit to reduce your cash to close and find a small rental, it certainly is possible. Of course, you can wait fifteen or even eighteen months to save more money if you would like. The takeaway here is not the amounts;

rather it is the idea that house hacking can enable you to save more money that can be used to buy rental properties.

ALERT

Traditional investment loans typically require 20–30 percent as down payment, but investors can use low- and no-money-down strategies to reduce the amount of cash they have to outlay. This can be tricky for newer investors and isn't recommended until investors have a bit more experience.

Even if someone does have the money to buy a rental property and therefore does not need the monthly savings from house hacking to save up the down payment, they might not be ready mentally. Buying a rental property can be intimidating and nerve-racking. After all, it is a very large purchase with a lot of responsibility, and can be potentially risky. These characteristics often lead to a situation where aspiring investors just learn, learn, learn and never take action. They get stuck in the learning phase. House hacking can get you over these hurdles. Famed investor Warren Buffett once said, "I don't look to jump over seven-foot bars; I look around for one-foot bars that I can step over." Traditional rental properties can be seen as the seven-foot bar Buffett is referring to, while a house hack is the one-foot bar. You can improve at something by stepping over the one-foot bars, then progress to seven-foot bars. Instead of only learning from books and podcasts, you can actually start taking action by buying a house hack and getting real-world, hands-on experience.

ESSENTIAL

Using house hacking as a stepping-stone to other investing strategies is why house hacking is often referred to as "landlording lite" or "landlording with training wheels." Similar to riding a bike, learning to house hack teaches you to become a landlord and/or real estate investor with as little barrier to entry as possible.

House hacking and traditional rental properties are not mutually exclusive, nor does either have to be done in a specific order. As has been explained in this chapter, someone typically house hacks *then* buys a traditional rental property. That is a great strategy, especially for new investors, but if you already own traditional rental properties, that does not mean that you can't also house hack. Your starting point may be different than someone else's, but ultimately, house hacking and buying traditional rentals are not opposites; they are actually even more powerful when combined.

Taking the Leap

If you did a bit of self-reflection, you would probably realize that many of the times you have been nervous in life have been because of lack of experience, lack of education, or uncertainty. In reality, uncertainty is a product of lacking experience and/or education—lack of education or experience leads to uncertainty, which leads to nervousness. This dynamic can apply to house hacking, since it may be your first real estate investment, but it is often more prevalent with other forms of real estate investing because you typically have more at stake and it is a bit more difficult—as Buffett would say, they are seven-foot bars. House hacking is a bit less nerve-racking because it is a "lite" version of real estate investing—it is a one-foot bar. You will still be nervous due to lack of experience, but since there is lower risk and a lower barrier to entry, it is easier to jump in and get started with little to no experience with house hacking than it is with other strategies.

ALERT

Making the leap into house hacking may be easier than buying a traditional rental because many people already have a bit of experience with a similar concept without realizing it. If you have ever rented an apartment and shared it with other people, you have experience implementing a concept that's quite similar to house hacking.

Once you have taken the leap into house hacking, you can build real experience and education that makes it much easier to jump into other forms of real estate investing. One of the first concepts you learned in this book was to build your team. Some new investors may think they do not have much to lose in this area, but they would be wrong. If you were to start out by jumping right into buying a rental, you may not know what makes for a good real estate agent, how to talk with property managers, or whom to call for repairs and maintenance. You may not even know you need a team, who those professionals are, or what skills they should have. By house hacking first, you will go through the process of finding, selecting, and working with a real estate agent. You may make mistakes, which you can learn from and then apply to your future real estate deals.

> **ESSENTIAL**
>
> Thousands of investors started by investing in traditional rental properties or possibly even more complex strategies. It absolutely can be done. House hacking isn't required to start investing in real estate, but it is a great option for many.

Know What You Are Looking For

A very common mistake among new real estate investors, house hacking or not, is not defining their target strategy and property type. Many try to start investing by simply saying they want to buy a rental property and searching the MLS. They end up frustrated because they "can't find any deals." In reality, they can't find a deal because they do not know what they are looking for. By house hacking first and implementing what you have learned in this book, you will know that you need to define which strategy you want to implement and which type of property you are looking for. With house hacking, you need to define if you are buying a multifamily property or if you are renting by the room—your strategy. Then you need to determine if you want a single-family house or a fourplex—your property type. By going through this as part of your house hacking experience, you will know that you need to do this for nearly any type of real estate investing you do. This will save you significant time, headaches, and potentially even money.

Analyze Your Numbers

Analyzing the numbers of a house hack deal is slightly different than it is for other types of real estate investing, but as a general process, it is similar. You need to determine the rental rates for your rental units, whether it is a single bedroom, a long-term rental unit, or a short-term rental. Then subtract all of your expenses, which also vary slightly but have similar general categories—operating expenses such as utilities, and maintenance and repairs, and then debt servicing. The amount that is left over is your profit. The details of each strategy differ, but having experience analyzing house hack deals, then seeing how your results differ from your analysis, will help you significantly when you want to start analyzing other real estate deals.

House hacking is not only about real estate or financial gains. It forces you to get your personal finances in order. It's a mindset shift. It is like training for a sporting event. You spend time training before the event, you put in the effort during the event based on your training, and then you are in better physical shape afterward because of it. The same goes for house hacking. You have to get your personal finances "in shape" before applying for a mortgage, then you use the effort you put into getting your personal finances in shape to get your mortgage and complete the purchase, then afterward you continue to reap the benefits. All the time, effort, and knowledge you gained from learning about and implementing the house hacking strategy completely shifts your mindset around money—it changes how you see and approach your personal finances.

Nerves Are Normal

Even for traditional home buyers who are not house hacking, the acquisition and mortgage process can be very overwhelming, especially if they have never done it before. The process is long and can be tedious, but it is not overly complex or difficult. However, there is a lack of experience and uncertainty, which leads to nervousness. If you have been through the acquisition and mortgage process or have spent time learning what it is like, you will almost definitely be less nervous than if you had never been through it. It's not because the process has changed; it's still the same. It's because there is far less uncertainty. You have more experience or education to reduce your uncertainty, you know which inspections are coming, how negotiating works, and which documents your lender will need, all of which reduces your nervousness.

The relatively minor requirements and tasks of purchasing real estate can also create nervousness or stress if you have never done them before, such as attending showings, reading inspection reports, and understanding what is important and what is not. This dynamic is not only present in real estate; it is present in everyday life too. Whether it is something you have not done before, something you do not know much about, or something that is ambiguous, you are going to be nervous.

> **ALERT**
>
> Being nervous does not mean you should not do something. In fact, doing hard things that you are nervous about is where you can make big changes in your life and grow. As long as you can identify its source, the presence of nervousness should excite you and show you that you are on the right path—all that's left is to push through.

How to Reduce Your Risk If House Hacking Doesn't Work

Doing something you have never done before, like house hacking, causes uncertainty and nervousness, but gaining experience and knowledge are not the only ways to reduce those feelings. Risk is another key factor in the uncertainty and nervousness equation. If there is a high level of perceived risk, you are likely to be more nervous. To solve this problem and reduce your nervousness or increase your chance of taking action, reduce your risk.

When it comes to real estate, most new investors are focused on finding and buying what they consider to be great deals. Of course, this is an important component, but arguably even more important is knowing and defining your exit strategy. You can buy a deal that seems great on the front end but is actually a disaster on the back end when you have to sell it.

Let's look at two different examples to illustrate this point. For the first situation, assume you find a deal that requires you to put in $48,000 of your capital and will provide you with $1,000 per month in net cash flow. That is after all expenses *and* putting money aside for reserves each month. Assume you found a second deal that also requires you to put in $48,000 of your cash and will provide you with $600 per month in net cash flow, also after all expenses and reserves. From a purely mathematical and financial perspective, the first situation seems much better. You earn 40 percent more cash flow per month and earn a 10 percent higher annual cash amount on return. That is where most new investors end their analysis and begin making their mistake.

What if the first property had some sort of special characteristic that kept you from selling it as quickly as a "normal" property in that area? What if it could not be used for any other type of real estate investing strategy? Meanwhile, the second property would sell very quickly, if it needed to be put up for sale, and has multiple other real estate investing strategies that would work with it. Which property is riskier? Most likely, property one is riskier than property two.

FACT

The increased risk of property one does not necessarily mean that you can't purchase that property instead of property two, but it is important to understand the different risk profiles and determine which one you are most comfortable with.

Let's break down the risk profiles of those two properties to fully understand why the first property is riskier than the second. In academic theory, risk is defined as volatility. However, in the real world, risk is the loss of capital. One of Warren Buffett's most famous quotes is "The first rule of investing is don't lose money. And the second rule of investing is don't forget the first rule." It is a simple idea, but it is powerful and highlights the importance of not losing money. You can simply say, without much consideration, that you are okay with one option over the other. You may be okay with not earning as much as possible for the safety it provides. Or, instead of thinking about it simply, you can think a bit more critically and consider the risk-adjusted return.

Risk-Adjusted Return

A risk-adjusted return is simply an investment return that takes into consideration the amount of risk being taken to earn that return amount. You cannot accurately compare two investment opportunities without considering the risk-adjusted return. In a vacuum, one investment may appear to be better because it provides a higher return, such as property one in the previous example. What is not considered, however, is that that investment opportunity has ten units of risk, while the other investment opportunity only has one unit of risk. Even though the second investment opportunity provides a lower return, it only has one-tenth of the risk, therefore it has a much higher risk-adjusted return.

> **ESSENTIAL**
>
> There is generally a correlation between risk and return. There are sometimes asymmetric risk-return opportunities, which means the risk is not correlated to the return as the relationship normally is, but it is more common for the risk to be increased with increased returns, even if you may not be able to easily see the increased risk.

The consideration for which option to take in a multi-option situation does not just end with risk-adjusted return. Everyone has a different risk tolerance, which is the amount of risk they are willing to take. Some individuals are afraid of taking risks, while others are risk seekers. The former would prefer a lower return in exchange for higher safety and lower risk, which is often known as being risk-averse, while the latter is willing to roll the dice and take a bigger risk. Naturally, most humans are inclined to be risk-averse because the pain of a loss is often considered to be more impactful than the good feeling from a positive return. The risk aversion is even stronger when the stakes become larger, and there are not many purchases larger than a house or other rental property for the average person.

Exit Strategies

Since most people have a natural inclination to be risk-averse, let's look at ways to reduce your risk when house hacking to ensure you do not get stuck in analysis and are unable to take action. The two best ways to reduce your risk when house hacking is by understanding your exit strategies and which other real estate investing strategies you could implement with this property. Since risk is the loss of capital, consider the ways you can lose capital with real estate investing. One way is by being forced to sell at an inopportune time. You may argue that it can also be from maintenance or repairs on the property. While this is true, prominent real estate investor Brandon Turner has discussed how most negative things that happen to real estate investments can be overcome by holding on to the property for long enough. Your hot water heater breaks, or you need a new roof, and those items make the investment unprofitable? If it provides net cash flow each month, it is only a matter of time, even if it takes a while, before the cash flow covers the losses and it becomes positive again. The important takeaway is to put yourself in a position where there is a very small probability that you would be forced to sell.

FACT

The term "exit strategy" is actually a bit misleading because it implies that you must exit the property or deal. In reality, however, an exit strategy can simply be a change from the current situation. It can be an exit from a property altogether, but it does not have to be.

You can lower the risk of being forced to sell at a bad time by implementing other strategies and having enough cash reserves. Frequently, owners are forced to sell because they cannot meet the debt service requirements.

If you set aside enough money in reserves, whether at the beginning of your purchase or through monthly savings, having enough money in reserves can cover your loan payments each month until you can stabilize the property again.

Common exit strategies include selling the property, refinancing, or implementing a new strategy. Why is "selling the property" an option? Wasn't it just explained that you shouldn't sell the property? Not quite. It was explained that you should put yourself in a situation where you can't be *forced* to sell the property when you do not want to. That is different than choosing to sell the property when you want to on your terms as one of your exit strategies. Also, even if you were forced to sell, that is still considered an exit. It may not be a good exit, which is what this chapter is teaching you how to do, but it would still remove you from the situation as long as you at least cover the outstanding loan balances.

If you were in a situation where you were being forced to sell by one lender or you needed capital to solve a problem, you may be able to refinance. This could stop the current lender from forcing a sale and, if it's a cash-out refinance, provide you the capital to complete the necessary repairs. Lenders usually force owners to sell their properties only if they are in some sort of distress, typically financial distress. If that is the case for you, it may be difficult to refinance with someone else. You may need to refer to Chapter 10 and choose a more creative option for refinancing. You can also only do a cash-out refinance if you have enough equity in the property at the time of the refinance. A refinance is considered an exit strategy because it removes you from your current negative situation.

> **ESSENTIAL**
>
> Traditional lenders typically only provide cash-out refinances if your loan-to-value (LTV) ratio is below 75–80 percent. In most cases, you would need to be quite a bit under the lender's threshold in order to make it worthwhile. If you are too close to their minimum LTV, the amount you receive as part of the cash-out will probably be negligible.

The ideal situation for an exit strategy is being able to pivot to a new strategy. A benefit of house hacking is its flexibility and versatility. Instead of selling, or even refinancing, you could pivot to a new strategy before running into issues, or to get yourself out of a problem. As long as you have satisfied the one-year occupancy requirement of most owner-occupied mortgages, you can pivot your house hack into a traditional rental, short-term rental, rent-by-the-room, or even a student rental. A single-family, duplex, triplex, or fourplex could all become traditional rentals rather than a house hack relatively simply by finding one more tenant to take the space you were occupying.

Similar to traditional rentals, you can turn your space into a short-term rental and even turn one or more of the other units into a short-term rental as well if it is unoccupied or if the tenant is leaving soon. Many investors are not aware that rent-by-the-room strategies are not just for house hacking. It is certainly possible, and often highly profitable, to implement a rent-by-the-room strategy. If you have a whole unit to yourself, you can fill that unit by using a rent-by-the-room strategy, or if you are already using this strategy, you can continue it by replacing yourself with a new tenant in the room you are vacating. If the property is located in an area where there are universities and colleges, you may also be able to transition the property to student housing.

Nearly all of these exit strategies and strategy pivoting are applicable to other forms of real estate investing. If you are not house hacking and instead own traditional rental properties, you could implement the refinance option or pivot to a different strategy, such as a short-term rental or rent-by-the-room. If you already have a short-term rental but want to go a different route, you can sell it or convert it to a different strategy, such as a student rental or a long-term traditional rental. These strategies of exiting and pivoting can be applied to nearly all residential real estate investing, even some small- to medium-sized apartment buildings.

Self-Reflection for Areas of Improvement

Ray Dalio, one of the most successful investors of all time, founder of one of the world's largest hedge funds, and a *New York Times* bestselling author, has two great quotes about mistakes. The first is "For every mistake that you learn from you will save thousands of similar mistakes in the future, so if you treat mistakes as learning opportunities that yield rapid improvements you should be excited by them. But if you treat them as bad things, you will make yourself and others miserable, and you won't grow." The second is "It is okay to make mistakes and unacceptable not to learn from them." Unfortunately, too many people are afraid of making mistakes and do not take the time to learn from them when they do make one.

To become a better investor and save yourself time and money, you must learn to embrace mistakes and how to learn from them. It is not enough to simply learn to not do something. Rather, you must learn why something failed, where it went wrong, why the outcome was bad, and how to do it differently next time. The most obvious situation with a house hack is in your deal analysis. If you run your numbers before purchasing the property and your actual results are significantly different, it is easy to see that something went wrong. But this is not where your variance analysis should end.

Even though other items and differences are harder to quantify, that does not mean they are not important to consider. After you have worked with your real estate agent through a transaction, you should spend time reflecting on the process. Were your standards met? Could it have been better? If so, how? What would you like to be different in a new agent, if you choose to use a new one? The same reflection process can and should be completed for each real estate professional as part of the team you build (see Chapter 5).

Similar to your deal analysis reflection, you should conduct a review process for your market research and the property type you choose. Is your analysis of the area accurate or different than you expected? Do you enjoy the property type you picked, or would you prefer a different one?

The reality is that all aspects of the process should be reviewed for areas of improvement. That includes the items listed previously, as well as making an offer, negotiating, getting financing, finding tenants, and everything in between. Mistakes are going to be made, even if you are a seasoned real estate investor. No two real estate transactions are the same, so even if you have experience in one area, that does not mean you know everything that could be thrown your way. You are going to make mistakes, but rather than seeing them as a negative thing and getting down on yourself, use them to drive change, improvement, and excitement. Become excited by knowing you can and will be better because of the negative thing that happened.

House hacking is simple, but isn't easy. It takes hard work, determination, and sacrifice, but when you look back on how it impacted your life, you will be thankful you did it. Enjoy the journey, and your newfound blueprint for achieving financial freedom.

APPENDIX A:
THE BUYING-A-HOME CHECKLIST

- ❏ Research the market
- ❏ Get preapproved
- ❏ Find a real estate agent
- ❏ Look at properties in your budget
- ❏ Send an offer to purchase; if your offer gets accepted…
- ❏ Schedule an inspection
- ❏ Get an appraisal
- ❏ Do a walk-through
- ❏ Close and execute purchase and sale
- ❏ Move in!

APPENDIX B:
MARKET RESEARCH

In Chapter 7, you learned about how to find the right market for your house hack. Use this space to make notes on different locations to figure out where you'd like to buy property.

Population Growth

LOCATION 1

_____

_____

_____

LOCATION 2

_____

_____

_____

LOCATION 3

_____

_____

_____

Income Growth

LOCATION 1

_____

_____

_____

LOCATION 2

_____

_____

_____

LOCATION 3

_____

_____

_____

Property Value Growth

LOCATION 1

_____

_____

_____

LOCATION 2

_____

_____

_____

LOCATION 3

_____

_____

_____

Crime Level

LOCATION 1

_____

_____

_____

LOCATION 2

_____

_____

_____

LOCATION 3

_____

_____

_____

Crime Change

LOCATION 1

_____

_____

_____

LOCATION 2

_____

_____

_____

LOCATION 3

_____

_____

_____

Job Growth

LOCATION 1

_____

_____

_____

LOCATION 2

_____

_____

_____

LOCATION 3

_____

_____

_____

APPENDIX C:
REAL ESTATE TEAM

In Chapter 5, you learned about the key relationships you need to form in order to be successful in house hacking. Keep track of these relationships and the contacts you make with the following form.

REAL ESTATE AGENT

Name: _____

Phone Number: _____

Email: _____

Notes: _____

LENDER

Name: _____

Phone Number: _____

Email: _____

Notes: _____

INSPECTOR/INSPECTION COMPANY

Name: _____

Phone Number: _____

Email: _____

Notes: _____

ATTORNEY

Name: _____

Phone Number: _____

Email: _____

Notes: _____

INSURANCE AGENT/BROKER

Name: _____

Phone Number: _____

Email: _____

Notes: _____

PROPERTY MANAGER

Name: _____

Phone Number: _____

Email: _____

Notes: _____

HANDYMAN

Name: _____

Phone Number: _____

Email: _____

Notes: _____

ELECTRICIAN

Name: _____

Phone Number: _____

Email: _____

Notes: _____

PLUMBER

Name: _____

Phone Number: _____

Email: _____

Notes: _____

HVAC INSTALLER/REPAIRER

Name: _____

Phone Number: _____

Email: _____

Notes: _____

CARPENTER

Name: _____

Phone Number: _____

Email: _____

Notes: _____

LANDSCAPER/LANDSCAPING COMPANY

Name: _____

Phone Number: _____

Email: _____

Notes: _____

LOCKSMITH

Name: _____

Phone Number: _____

Email: _____

Notes: _____

VIRTUAL ASSISTANT

Name: _____

Phone Number: _____

Email: _____

Notes: _____

APPENDIX D:
PROPERTY SEARCH NOTES

During your search, it's likely you'll look at more than one property. Use these pages to make notes on each of the properties you look at so you can compare them side by side.

PROPERTY #1

Address:

_____

Listing Price: _____

Pros:

_____

_____

_____

_____

_____

Cons:

_____

_____

_____

_____

_____

PROPERTY #2

Address:

_____

Listing Price: _____

Pros:

_____

_____

_____

_____

_____

Cons:

_____

_____

_____

_____

_____

PROPERTY #3

Address:

_____

Listing Price: _____

Pros:

_____

_____

_____

_____

_____

Cons:

_____

_____

_____

_____

_____

PROPERTY #4

Address:

_____

Listing Price: _____

Pros:

_____

_____

_____

_____

_____

Cons:

_____

_____

_____

_____

_____

PROPERTY #5

Address:

_____

Listing Price: _____

Pros:

_____

_____

_____

_____

_____

Cons:

_____

_____

_____

_____

_____

PROPERTY #6

Address:

_____

Listing Price: _____

Pros:

_____

_____

_____

_____

_____

Cons:

_____

_____

_____

_____

_____

PROPERTY #7

Address:

_____

Listing Price: _____

Pros:

_____

_____

_____

_____

_____

Cons:

_____

_____

_____

_____

_____

PROPERTY #8

Address:

_____

Listing Price: _____

Pros:

_____

_____

_____

_____

_____

Cons:

_____

_____

_____

_____

_____

PROPERTY #9

Address:

_____

Listing Price: _____

Pros:

_____

_____

_____

_____

_____

Cons:

_____

_____

_____

_____

_____

PROPERTY #10

Address:

_____

Listing Price: _____

Pros:

_____

_____

_____

_____

_____

Cons:

_____

_____

_____

_____

_____

APPENDIX E:
NEW HOME CHECKLIST

As you learned in Chapter 5, once a property is under contract the next step is to get an inspection and schedule a walk-through. The inspector should put together a report and check out all the elements of the house, but it's not a bad idea for you to take a look through the house and make sure everything is as you are expecting. Here's a list to help you keep track of everything you have looked at and/or tested out.

- ☐ Doors
- ☐ Doorbell
- ☐ Driveway
- ☐ Deck/Porch/Patio
- ☐ Garage Doors
- ☐ Garbage and Recycling
- ☐ House Number
- ☐ Mailbox
- ☐ Outdoor Lights
- ☐ Paint and Trim
- ☐ Sidewalks
- ☐ Siding
- ☐ Traffic Noise
- ☐ Windows
- ☐ Chimney
- ☐ Gutters/Downspouts
- ☐ Roof
- ☐ Garage Ceiling
- ☐ Garage Lights
- ☐ Yard Drainage

- ☐ Fences/Gates
- ☐ Retaining Wall
- ☐ Shed
- ☐ Sprinklers
- ☐ Pool
- ☐ Fireplaces
- ☐ Carbon Monoxide Detector
- ☐ Smoke Alarm
- ☐ Kitchen Appliances
- ☐ Kitchen Coils and Vents
- ☐ Water Filters
- ☐ Drains and Garbage Disposal
- ☐ Pipes
- ☐ Faucets and Toilets
- ☐ Showerheads
- ☐ Caulking in Bathroom
- ☐ Main Shut-Off Valve
- ☐ Electrical System
- ☐ HVAC
- ☐ Water Heater
- ☐ Air Ducts and Vents
- ☐ Air Filters
- ☐ Foundation
- ☐ Drafts
- ☐ Locks on Windows and Doors
- ☐ Lighting
- ☐ Security Cameras and Alarm Systems

APPENDIX F:
CALCULATING INCOME

You can use the space here to determine what monthly income you need to bring in to reach your goals. As you learned in Chapter 2, total monthly rental income minus mortgage expense equals gross profit. (Don't forget, you'll need to make sure you are putting aside reserves from the monthly gross profit to cover maintenance, repairs, and capital expenditures [CAPEX] when those issues arise.)

APPENDIX G: TENANT APPLICATIONS

In Chapter 11, you learned about what to look for when evaluating a tenant's application. This table can help keep you organized as you work through this. Note that these aren't required steps in choosing a tenant. As the landlord, you determine what is most important to you.

	Applicant A	Applicant B	Applicant C	Applicant D
Credit Score or Debt-to-Income Ratio				
Background Check				
Employment History				
References				

INDEX